> *Suffer little children to come unto me, and forbid them not: for of such is the kingdom of heaven.*—Jesus

"Because they are not shackled by tradition, ritual, or dogma, the retarded can enjoy the simplest, most basic kind of faith.

"When a middle-aged man with a child's mentality was asked what he had learned in church that week, he replied unhesitatingly, 'God loves me!'

"This is the foundation of the Gospel message.

"We pray that the reader will find encouragement to share his faith with those who will remain forever as little children."

1

LOOK AT ME, PLEASE LOOK AT ME

Dorothy Clark & Jane Dahl
Lois Gonzenbach

David C. Cook Publishing Co.
850 NORTH GROVE AVENUE • ELGIN, IL 60120
In Canada: David C. Cook Publishing (Canada) Ltd., Weston, Ontario M9L 1T4

LOOK AT ME, PLEASE LOOK AT ME

First printing, June 1973
Second printing, November 1973

Printed in the United States of America
Library of Congress Catalog Card Number: 73-76698

ISBN 0-912692-11-1

TO OUR FAMILIES
for love,
for guidance,
and
for encouragement

CONTENTS

FAITH

13 Look at Me, Please Look at Me
20 Frankly Fearful
27 Come to Me
29 Tick . . . Tick . . . Tick . . .
33 Fringe Benefits
35 Oh, Holy Night!
39 Once Around the Floor to "Faith of Our Fathers"
41 The Little Shall Lead Them
44 Glad to Be God's Guests

HOPE

48 A Potential for Loveliness
53 Bend Down to God's Level
55 This Little Piggy Went to Market
57 Not Again!
60 It's What's up Front that Counts
65 This Old House
69 From the Mouths of Babes
71 The Decision

LOVE

79 Stewed Tomatoes
84 Amen—Ahead and at Last!
88 Right In, Right On
91 Only a Promise of Love
93 The Retrieved and Relieved
97 That's Where It's at
99 Help Todd Now
103 Shalom—But Hanukkah!
106 Clothes Make the Woman
109 How Do You Know I Love You?
113 The Reluctant Volunteer
120 A Look at Discipline

PREFACE

I HAVE A GIFT for you. Misshapen, torn, and tied loosely with twine, it is a large and cumbersome box. I place it in your hesitant hands. You smile as if to ask, "Is this a joke?"

As I nod encouragement, you tug at the twine. It breaks and the wrapping flutters to the floor. Slowly you lift the cover. A delightful fragrance emerges from the box. Pushing aside the layers of tissue you discover a bouquet of roses. They are deep red and just beginning to unfold.

Your face brightens. You lift the flowers. Inhale their perfume. Touch the cool, soft velvet petals.

"Thank you," your words tinged with wonder, leave an unspoken Why?

Had you rejected your gift because of the ugly wrapping, you would have missed the beauty of the real gift inside.

The mentally and physically handicapped are often like your package; difficult to look upon, unattractive, and in some instances even repulsive. But if you look past childlike minds and damaged bodies, you will discover God-created men, women, boys, and girls who are waiting to be wanted, to be accepted, to be loved.

You turn away, shaking your head. You say it is impossible to love and accept someone you normally would draw away from. You are right. But with Christ in you it is not impossible. He will accept and love them through you.

As you turn this page and read these stories of true incidents, you may find still another gift meant just for you. If your life has been touched by a retarded child, the gift is Encouragement. If you have doubted the retarded can be reached, the gift is Assurance. If you have searched unsuccessfully for ways to share your faith with the handicapped, the gift is Inspiration. And if through fear and misconception you have avoided involvement with them, the gift is Love.

I pray you will receive whatever gift God has for you.

Walnut Creek, California   DOROTHY CLARK

Look at Me, Please Look at Me is a collection of true incidents evolving from the work of Dorothy Clark and Jane Dahl with the mentally handicapped in worship services, Christmas pageants, and various field trips.

Mrs. Clark was the director-teacher of the program for ten years and Mrs. Dahl was one of her assistants. Mrs. Gonzenbach, while not involved in the program itself, has lent her talents in advising and in the writing of this book.

All names of the children have been changed to protect their identities.

1

LOOK AT ME, PLEASE LOOK AT ME

STUBBY FINGERS gripped the Bible inches away from the man's thick glasses. Although he read well enough, it was obvious he read without understanding. His speech was slow, labored, and lacking in normal voice inflection.

What's the point of all this, I asked myself, looking around the room.

Suddenly I shuddered as something heavy began pounding, thud . . . thud . . . thud! There on the stage, a large boy lay flat on his stomach, his feet and legs rising and falling like an enormous pendulum, thud . . . thud!

As if in accompaniment, chairs scraped against the floor, voices called indistinguishable words, restless people moved about the room, and an eerie howling intermittently pierced the air.

"And this is supposed to be a Christian education class!" I muttered.

As the man's voice droned on, barely audible now above the increasing racket, I wondered how I got into this mess. Actually, the process had taken almost two years. During that time, Margaret, a friend, had invited me to visit this class for the retarded many times. I resisted from the beginning. From the beginning, she persisted. Then early that week, she called—not with another invitation—but this time, with an ultimatum: "Dorothy, you're coming this once to get me off your back!" We were both surprised when I suddenly agreed.

Now, here I sat in the front row, no way prepared for this experience. In the first place, Margaret always referred to these people as "children." What a shock it was to discover she was referring to a physical age span of four to sixty-seven years and a mental age span of eighteen months to eleven years. Then, too, she had somehow forgotten to mention that many of the "children" were also physically handicapped.

As the service progressed, I retreated further and further within myself, less and less able to keep in focus. My only point of contact was a young man sitting next to me; when he stood I stood; when he sat I sat; and, when he sang I hummed. The rest of the time I wrestled with an irresistible urge to bolt from the room.

The service finally ended but the noise didn't. As if marking cadence, the thudding from the stage continued while thirty children filed from the worship center to several class areas within the large room. I watched and waited, purposely holding back. The boys' class I was assigned to formed a circle with their chairs. When they were seated, I carefully placed my chair on the perimeter—close enough to observe but not close enough to be included. The boys were quick to remedy my error. They simply enlarged the circle to include me.

Thanks alot, I thought, that's all I need!

When a volunteer introduced me as a visitor, nine pairs of eyes turned in my direction. What do they see, I wondered—my fear, pity, or just a nervous smile? I began to relax when class activities drew their attention away from me. To my surprise the boys' conversation was enthusiastic and happy. After a short interlude, the volunteer's voice cut through the pleasant commotion, "Now we'll have our thank-you prayer time."

Suddenly I was in sharp focus for the first time that afternoon. Dear Lord, I thought, this is too much! What do they have to be thankful for? In that moment of concern for the children, rather than myself, I realized I had been thinking only of *my* feelings, *my* fear, *my* inability to share myself. "Lord, forgive me," I whispered.

As if in answer to my plea, the boys prayed around the circle—each in his own way thanking God for me! Hank, the young man who sat next to me earlier, closed, "Please, God, send Dorothy back."

The prayer time over, the nine pairs of eyes were fixed again on me. As each child searched my face, he seemed to be asking, Will she look at me? Really at me? Please, let her look at me! Hank reached out and gently touched my hand. Then I did look at him—really looked at him— and I saw the son that could have been mine!

Ever since our little damaged son was born prematurely many years before, my husband and I seldom spoke of him. He was not the first child my body rejected too soon to live. After miraculously recovering from what doctors called "terminal cancer," I had several miscarriages. With each tiny life lost, I became more rebellious and determined to have my own way.

Over the years, the scars from the cancer healed. But the wound caused by my despair at never bearing a child did not. It was a wound I would not allow even the Lord to deal with.

Now, as I looked at Hank, I wondered, Is God showing me that His will, though difficult, *was* best? Oh, Margaret, I dismayed, without knowing it you've forced me to look at a part of my life that was buried long ago.

Later, at home again, I stretched out on the carpet before the fireplace. I watched the flames skip across the logs and burst into color. My mind kept returning to that moment when Hank prayed, "Please, God, send Dorothy back!" "Please, God," I prayed, "don't send me back!"

The next morning, determined not to let my mind dwell on my experiences of the previous day, I got ready to attend my weekly Bible class. I looked forward to hearing Miss A. Wetherell Johnson, founder of Bible Study Fellowship, whose faith drew me week after week.

This day I found my usual place in a front pew. When the opening hymn and prayer were concluded, I glanced up expectantly as Miss Johnson stepped to the podium. She placed her notes before her. Then without comment, she leaned forward, her eyes intently searching each face. Finally, in a clear voice she asked, "Lady, what are *you* doing for the Lord?" Suddenly all the other women vanished into the woodwork. She was speaking only to me! There were just three of us—Miss Johnson, my Lord, and me.

Although she had already had a great impact on my life, her message that day set my mind and soul on fire. She spoke of serving the Lord in such exciting and challenging terms, I found myself promising God I would do His work. All He needed to do was show me what He wanted, and I would do it!

Spiritually filled to overflowing, I arrived home several hours later to a ringing telephone. "Dorothy, this is Margaret," my friend explained. "Our teacher has left unexpectedly. Would you consider teaching next week's lesson?" After a long pause, she continued, "Dorothy, are you there?"

"Yes, I'm here," I answered, "and NO I can't teach your handicapped class! Margaret, you promised, if I visited that one time, you'd get off my back."

"I know," she interrupted, "but I didn't count on being without a teacher so suddenly. Please pray about it." And with that she hung up.

I knelt by my bed, angry and confused. "Lord," I poured out my heart, "please, I'll do anything else—but *not* this." All at once my promise of that morning came back to haunt me. "Okay, Lord," I sighed. "If you want me to, I'll teach this one time. But if You want me to do anything more with these children, You'll have to show me in a way I can understand—without question or doubt!"

The next week arrived too soon, and with it the dreaded day. I was nervous and apprehensive as I entered the church hall. My worst fears were realized immediately. The children were in a state of noisy excitement. From the stage came the familiar thud . . . thud . . . thud of the week before. As I sat down, I overheard two volunteers discussing the young man responsible for the constant thudding. It seemed he had been lying spread-eagle, engaged in his favorite pastime since the program first began. Oh, no, I thought, that would be over two years! Nothing they attempted proved successful in getting him off the stage. Great, I thought!

When the worship service began that day, I sat with hands folded to control the shaking. Soon it was time for the lesson. I rose and walked to the microphone. Thud . . . thud . . . thud . . . matched my steps. How can I teach, I moaned silently, with that going on to distract me? Lord, help me! Nonchalantly I rolled the large blackboard across the floor until it blocked the view of the lone, prone kicker on stage. Now he was out of the class' sight and the class was out of his sight. Almost at once the rhythm of his kicking changed noticeably. As I turned to face the group, the noise level seemed to rise higher.

Surveying the chaotic scene before me, I put it again to the Lord. "You're going to have to do it all, Lord. In the first place, I don't have anything to give—nothing that would really make a difference in their lives. And even if I did, they'd never hear it above all this racket. You led me into this situation, Lord. If You want me to proceed, please bring quiet to this room—somehow, someway!"

Then, bowing my head, I prayed aloud, "Dear Lord, we claim Your promise that where two or three are gathered together in Your name, there You will be also. Thank You, Lord. Amen."

As I concluded, there was a shuffling sound behind me. Someone was descending the stairs from the stage. I dared not turn to look. Slowly the large boy came into my peripheral vision, then proceeded to cross in front of me to a vacant chair in the front row. He sat down, folded his hands in his lap, and began to rock to and fro.

I was so engrossed in his historic exodus that I failed to notice that a sudden stillness encompassed the room.

Slowly it dawned on me—no scraping of chairs, no people wandering about, no voices calling, and no eerie howling. Every child was giving me his full attention!

God had answered my prayers for direction and help beyond anything I could have anticipated. As I stood looking into the eagerly waiting faces, I found myself wanting to shout, "*Look at me*—and I'll look at you! *Look at me*—we'll love each other! *Please*—I'll never turn away again! *Look at me*—I have something wonderful to share! It is *love,* God's abundant love!"

That was ten years ago. In the intervening years, I have not seen twisted bodies healed or damaged minds restored. But I have seen far greater miracles—peace replace fear, faith replace frustration, hope replace despair, and love replace loneliness.

So then faith cometh by hearing,
and hearing by the word of God
(Romans 10: 17 *).*

DOES A CRIPPLED MIND and misshapen body render one incapable of experiencing the love of God? Can one so handicapped claim the assurance of a Heavenly Father who cares about him personally?

We believe that whenever communication is possible, even the more severely retarded can be helped to know God. The way may be long and discouraging with little or no evidence of progress. The teacher or parent may reach the depths of his own faith and still feel he has not succeeded. That of course is the point—he cannot. Only God can make Himself a reality. We need only to be His faithful tools, depending confidently on His infinite power. Romans 12: 3 states that it is God Himself who assigns each measure of faith. Surely then He will make provision for those who need Him so.

Because they are not shackled by tradition, ritual, or dogma, the retarded can enjoy the simplest, most basic kind of faith. When a middle-aged man with a child's mentality was asked what he had learned in church that week, he replied unhesitatingly, "God loves me!" This is the foundation of the Gospel message.

In the following accounts of true incidents, we pray that the reader will find encouragement to share his faith with those who will forever remain as little children.

2

FRANKLY FEARFUL

THE CHILD'S penetrating glance searched my face as he thrust his small hand into mine. "I'm Tommy," he introduced himself. "Do you know Jesus?"

Wow, I thought, these kids don't mess around! "Why, yes, as a matter of fact I do."

I was one of a group of ministers who were in the process of getting acquainted with some of the twelve retarded adults and children who had been brought from their school to a centrally located church for a workshop.

"That's good," my new little friend continued, "most of us do, too. 'Cept maybe Sybil and Mike." He gestured toward the small yellow bus that was still unloading. "Sybil gets scared and lonesome at night and won't let anybody touch her. Mike, he can't walk good. He says, 'How come Jesus won't fix my legs?' "

I couldn't let the opportunity pass. "Tommy, why do you think Jesus hasn't fixed Mike's legs?"

"I don't know. He fixes some people. Some He don't. But He loves *everybody!*" A grin spread across the pixy face as he dashed off across the lawn, stopping momentarily to wave.

As I watched the retreating figure, I recalled how I had dreaded this day—a day I literally prayed myself into. A concern for the spiritual needs of the handicapped had been growing within me. It became so persistent that I asked my secretary to pray with me for ways I might help in this needy area. Soon came the invitation to this workshop. "It's not safe to pray," my secretary said as she handed it to me, "unless you're ready for an answer!"

Now I was here, along with ten ministers from other churches and denominations—hesitant, awkward, and fearful of doing or saying the wrong thing. But at least my confidence was returning, thanks to Tommy. Perhaps the day would not be the disaster I anticipated.

As Tommy's figure zipped around a building and out of sight, I shook myself loose from daydreaming, and looked for someone else with whom to get acquainted. After all, that was why I was here.

I noticed a woman sitting alone. Her attention seemed fixed upon one of the plants in the garden. I introduced myself and asked if I might sit with her. She nodded, continuing to give the plant her full attention.

I broke the silence: "Do you know what kind of flower that is?"

"It's a camellia," she replied turning toward me. Appearing to be about twenty, she took a fleeting look into my eyes, then turned back to the plant. "Did you see the buds?" she asked. "The color is beginning to show."

"You know a lot about flowers, don't you?" I encouraged.

"They're like people," her words surprised me. "They need someone to watch out for them; this one needs water."

I felt my hesitation and fear diminish as she spoke. "They need someone to watch out for them; this one needs water." Her words echoed in my mind like a message from the Lord. "These little lambs need your care. Give them the Living Water."

Responding to her horticultural evaluation, I said, "You're right. See? The leaves are beginning to wilt."

"What's your name?" she asked me.

"Bob."

"Mr. Bob?"

"Maybe you'd like to call me Pastor Bob," I suggested.

"You didn't tell me your name yet."

"Jill. Why did you come today? You and the other men?"

"To meet you and the others and maybe start a worship service or Sunday school like you have," I explained. "Jill, when it's time for the worship service, may I sit with you? This is all new to me."

"Yes," she said, "see you later."

Having been dismissed, I got up and walked away.

"Bob! Wait a minute!" It was Dave, another minister. Pulling up beside me, he said, "Let's compare notes. What are the kids like that you've contacted?"

"Well, I've only talked to two so far," I began. "Tommy, a little guy, nearly ran me down to find out if I knew Jesus. The young woman I just left gave me a lesson in horticulture, explaining that plants are like people. How about you, Dave?"

"Well, to be honest, I didn't go near the bus when it first arrived. Just stood off to the side watching things happen. The one that interested me most was the big guy over there. He's my height, over six feet. Someone said he's only fifteen! Anyway, he was so gentle with the little tot, the one with the braces. When I tried to talk to him all he wanted to know was, 'What's to eat? I'm hungry!' " Dave shook his head and smiled. "The other young man I met was James. He told me he was glad I'd come to worship with him. Then he showed me his first 'paycheck.' From the look of it, it had been folded and unfolded a hundred times. I understand the kids have jobs at the school which they do without pay—in other words, it's their responsibility toward the care of their home and family. But here was this check for five dollars for cleaning the toilets in the dorms for a month. Someone apparently donated five dollars from his own pocket to help James feel he had accomplished something worthwhile."

"Dave," I interrupted, "it's evident these kids are just like yours and mine. Each has his own identity, personality. They are more like our own kids than they are unlike them."

Nodding in agreement, my friend added, "And I have a feeling they aren't confused with our differences in theology. They sure aren't collecting many worldly goods at five dollars a month, either!"

We decided to talk to other children before the service began and headed out in opposite directions. I had taken but a dozen steps when a heavy blow on my back caught me off guard. The forward thrust carried me into a group of ladies. Anger welled up within me. The young man responsible hurried around in front of me, grabbed my hand, and began shaking it vigorously.

I had the urge to shake him in return—but he was bigger! I apologized to the women with the youth still attached to my right hand.

"Johnny," one of the ladies scolded, "you know that was too hard! Tell the gentleman you're sorry."

At once Johnny hung his head and eased his iron grip.

"We're sorry," the lady said turning to me, "Johnny must have taken a liking to you."

Whew, I thought, that kind of affection I can do without!

"Many of the children," she went on to explain, "can't express themselves verbally. So they act out what they have to say."

At this point I was grateful Johnny *did* like me! Just then he let go of my hand, reached into his pocket and produced a snapshot. He pushed it toward me. It was a family scene—the focal point a new baby. Johnny had chosen me to share something special with. My anger melted. But what was this I felt in its place? Love? Love!

As time for the worship service drew near, I excused myself and, giving Johnny's hand a farewell shake, looked around for Jill. She was standing near the door waiting for me.

We entered the room. My congregation should see this, I mused as she chose a place for us in the front row.

The service began with a young man and woman singing "Great Is Thy Faithfulness." The familiar words of this favorite hymn dispelled the last vestiges of tension, fear, and apprehension—not just for me; I sensed the entire congregation was similarly blessed. I looked around. The other ministers were sitting happily among the children. We were Christians worshiping our Lord together.

There were times in the service so quiet that I could almost hear my heart beating. Other times there would be a burst of applause, not out of irreverence, but in spontaneous appreciation of something beautiful.

The children prayed for one another, and for special needs in their own lives. And then the lesson began—what a revelation in simplicity; yet it had depth and meaning. The teacher, Mrs. Clark, used a method that reminded me of Christ's teaching. She used familiar objects and materials in simple illustrations. Then, interacting with the people, she applied His message to their lives.

This day's lesson pointed out the worth of each individual, regardless of his mental or physical wholeness. Mrs. Clark began by using a variety of brushes and discussing their uses. She involved the children by having those wanting to participate come forward to take a brush from a large basket, which she jiggled mysteriously. When the last student had chosen a brush, Mrs. Clark asked, "Mary, let's pretend you and I are kitchen helpers. I'll clean the stove while you scrub the floor. Use the brush you have, okay?"

Mary's face was a study in perplexity. "Are you kidding?" she asked as she looked at the toothbrush in her hand.

Then through a series of questions and statements, Mrs. Clark involved the entire class in giving reasons why the toothbrush was not a good tool for scrubbing the floor. Some of the children's statements were very direct and reflected a feeling rather than a reason, "Dumb!" . . . "Silly!" But others showed an understanding of the point being made. "It would take too long." . . . "You'd have to work harder." . . . "It wouldn't do a good job."

"All right," Mrs. Clark interrupted at last, "you've convinced me. Let's throw the brush away!"

"No!" was the explosive reply.

"But why not?" she countered. "It's not good for the floor."

"You need it for your teeth!" they called, dismayed at her lack of comprehension.

After repeating this routine with two other brushes, she began her final remarks.

"It's not the toothbrush's fault that it can't do a good job on the floor. It can't choose how it should be used. People made the toothbrush and all these other brushes, too. People made the brushes all different sizes, shapes, and colors. They made the brushes to do different jobs. Each brush is useful, helpful, and important. Each has its own special job to do."

Mrs. Clark continued as she laid the brushes aside and walked down the aisle. "Just as people made the brushes—God made us! Each of us is different—different in color, size, and what we are able to do. God has created us with a special purpose. And He has a plan for each of our lives."

She returned to the worship center and took a stack of photographs from an envelope. As she placed the picture of each child around the large painting of Christ, she made a comment about him. "God has given George the ability to read, so he can help those of us who can't read." . . . "God has given Donna a beautiful singing voice to make others happy." . . . "God has given Tim strong arms to help with the wheelchairs." It was apparent a great deal of preparation had gone into this part of the lesson. As each child heard his name and some glowing remark about himself, his face glowed in return. It was a happy time for everyone.

In her conclusion, Mrs. Clark asked us to repeat a verse from Romans which was printed on the blackboard: God has made each one different. We are each useful and important, no two of us are the same. Each of us has his own special purpose in God's family.

DANIEL J. BEHNKE

The children prepared to depart. Standing in a group on the sidewalk, we were smiling now, and relaxed, completely enjoying our new friends. We waved and called good-bye until the bus dipped out of sight.

Then Mrs. Clark invited us back inside for a time of sharing and evaluation. We arranged our chairs in a circle and began. "This morning," a minister from Antioch spoke, "all I could give was pity. They didn't need my pity. This afternoon, I found myself giving them love."

My friend Dave was next. "I wish Sunday mornings in my church had some of the enthusiasm and joy I saw here today. These children really enjoyed themselves, in spite of their severe handicaps."

I listened as one minister after another expressed his belief that God was leading him to begin an interdenominational worship service for the retarded. Then, I felt compelled to speak, "I was frankly fearful when I arrived this morning," I began. "But as in your lesson with the brushes, Mrs. Clark, God used several children to do specific jobs—on me! Tommy gave me the confidence to be open to the possibility of an outreach to the retarded. God used Jill to show me I was needed. Her understanding and concern for others brushed away many of my misconceptions and doubts. Then last, but not least, God used Johnny to show me I could love—in spite of myself. Johnny's bristles were the stiffest. It takes abrasiveness sometimes, I guess, to uncover love." I waited, but there was no response.

"I'm definitely going to reach out to the retarded," I continued, "and, with God's help, each child He gives me will know, through my efforts, that his life has value; that he has worth—as a person to other people, and as a spiritual being to God."

As my brother ministers nodded in agreement, I felt the unmistakable stirring of adventure. God was leading us into a new dimension of our ministries—and it was exciting.

3

COME TO ME

CHILDREN JOCKEYED good naturedly for first place in the chow line as the fragrance of lilacs mingled with the aroma of hot dogs roasting on an open grill. Overhead an early summer sun shared its warmth.

On the outskirts of the festivities sat a lone figure on a shaded bench. She was small for her nineteen years and her head was crowned with a mop of curly hair. Humming softly to herself, she surveyed the picnic activities.

Two of the women from church saw the lonely girl, approached, and stood before her. They were new to the program—unsure of themselves, yet eager to interact with the children.

"What's your name?" one asked shyly.

"Janet," was the quick reply.

"This is a nice school," the other ventured optimistically. There was no response.

For several minutes the women tried to engage the young girl in small talk, but weather, current tv programs, and favorite foods failed to interest her. There was a long, awkward silence. The women were wondering how to excuse themselves gracefully when a question was suddenly shot at them from the bench.

"And what," asked Janet boldly, "has the Lord done for you?"

"We were completely unprepared for such a question,"

they later exclaimed, "and we couldn't think of one thing!"

In desperation they turned the question back on its originator, "What has the Lord done for you, Janet?"

A smile broke across the small, oval face.

"He gives me rest," she replied confidently.

Lunch was announced and everyone moved toward the heavily laden tables. The two women, needing time to absorb and reflect, sat down on the empty bench. "Rest," she said—the sense of peace within—the elusive goal of a generation addicted to artificial tranquility. In Janet's smiling face they saw the source of her contentment— the Lord.

It took the women only a short time to learn that in matters of the Spirit the line between normalcy and retardation can sometimes be so fine that it becomes indefinable. And they knew this was one of those times.

4

TICK . . . TICK . . . TICK . . .

A DROP OF PERSPIRATION wandered along the tense and knotted muscles of my hot, sticky back. I looked around the rapidly filling sanctuary. The thought that six hundred people would be occupying the pews did nothing to relieve my apprehension.

"I feel like a new recruit on the bomb squad about to disarm my first bomb," I moaned inwardly.

I could almost hear the ticking.

When Dorothy asked me to take her place that evening, I was too shocked to protest. Anyway, she had already arranged with the school for the children to attend the performance of Handel's *Messiah*. There was nothing for me to do but say yes. It was easy for her— she was home sick in bed, but here I was sitting in the front row with the twelve wiggly, talkative, excited children. As far as I was concerned it was doomsday. Tick . . . tick . . .

People were walking quietly down the aisles, taking their seats with as little commotion as possible. An air of hushed anticipation replaced the usual recognition of friends and quiet conversation. There was a real feeling of worship . . .

"I have to go to the bathroom!"

There was Ann standing straight and tall announcing to the far reaches of the balcony that she needed to leave the room. The house mother and father who were accompanying the children remained composed and smiling. Apparently they didn't realize the seriousness of the situation. Ann, grinning and waving, was led down the aisle. Tick . . .

I looked at my watch and was aghast at the half hour left before the ritual of tuning the instruments would begin. This meant with the hour and half program, we would be trapped there sitting for two hours. Dorothy's confidence in the children was admirable, but this was too much. What was expected of them this night was without doubt beyond their emotional and physical limits.

Pastor Stoddard was busy in the empty choir loft making a last minute inspection of the amplification and recording equipment. I wondered what would happen if he looked out into the audience and saw the children sitting there front and center. Although he loved them, he "knew" them, too—their short attention span and the unexpected and sometimes uncontrollable nature of their behavior.

Well, I didn't have long to wonder. As Pastor, his handsome features composed and confident, skipped sprightly down the stairs and was about to slip out through the exit, he made a quick glancing appraisal of the audience. Without any visible immediate effect, his eyes swept across the dear happy faces in the front row. He had taken a full two steps through the doorway when suddenly it hit him! He froze, then slowly turned for another look. His expression mirrored my thoughts— impossible! incredible! He continued on his way but now trance-like and plodding. I knew that somehow, somewhere within seconds he would be on his knees.

There was a slight altercation between two children down the row from me. Heads were turning and eyebrows jumping as more of the audience became aware of special guests. The housefather motioned things were under control, but I knew it was only temporary.

The choir members were entering and taking their

places. The musicians arranged music on the shiny stands and readied their instruments. Mr. Harmon, the director, took his place on the small wooden platform in front of the orchestra. I watched him smiling and nodding as he raised his baton. Suddenly I was gripped with a horrible thought. The children, always enthusiastic and responsive, were used to applauding whenever something pleased them. In our special worship service we never restrained this gesture of appreciation. What if they suddenly broke into loud handclapping after one of the lovely, moving solos? I quickly got the attention of the housefather and mouthed the warning, "Tell the kids not to clap." He nodded and passed the word just as the opening notes filled the sanctuary. Tick . . . tick . . . tick . . .

Minute by minute of the next hour and a half I could feel the silent ticking like a giant pulse within me. I stiffened in expectation of the worst after each number but not one child made a sound! It was as if God laid His hand on their shoulders and His finger against their lips. Their faces were flushed and damp under the strain of being still, but I could tell from their expressions they were enjoying the beautiful music.

I was limp by the end of the program. Pastor Stoddard showed the effects of the evening, too. He had kept a wary eye on us most of the performance. After giving the benediction, he broke his precedent of quietly leaving the sanctuary and came to our pew to vigorously shake hands with each child. They seemed to think nothing of being singled out in this fashion and smiled at him adoringly. I could guess that with each handshake he was saying a silent "thank-you."

Later I watched the children load into the small school bus. They were waving good-bye as the bus pulled around the corner and out of sight. I stood alone in the empty parking lot. The night was cool and sweet around me.

It was late. Time passed unnoticed as I lingered. Overhead stars shimmered like jewels in a velvet setting.

"How vast is God's domain," I thought, "yet He was here—right here—tonight!"

A miracle had happened. And God in His compassionate wisdom allowed resisting, doubtful me to be a part of it.

> *When I consider thy heavens, the work of thy fingers, the moon and the stars, which thou hast ordained; What is man, that thou art mindful of him? and the son of man, that thou visitest him? (Psalm 8: 3, 4).*

5

FRINGE BENEFITS

ONE AFTERNOON as the children sang a hymn, some in discernible words, others in sounds and noises, my eyes swept across the group. Each familiar face reflected an eager innocence peculiar to the retarded.

There was Wil with the battered sports section of a newspaper beneath his arm. Against his waiting ear he pressed a silent transistor radio, long in need of batteries.

Farther along the row sat Paul and Jill holding hands. Their eyes embraced each other with a look of love.

Behind them Sammy rocked his chubby body to and fro on the lap of a grimacing helper.

My glance then slipped across Helen's face to Timmy—then back to Helen. Something was wrong. The usually smiling young woman sat pensive and preoccupied. "You're very quiet, Helen. Is something the matter?" I asked when the service was over.

Pushing her blond braids over her shoulders, she replied, "Don't worry, Dorothy. I've been troubled about the way I am, but I've given it to the Lord, and He is giving me a real peace about it. He's helping me accept myself as I am." In her words was the familiar mix of joy and pain.

Helen's intelligence, that of an eleven-year-old, is enough for her to know she is not normal. Deep frustration and agony are common companions to such understanding. Yet her face broke into a smile as she told me of turning to the Lord for comfort—and receiving it. Her new understanding and acceptance of self in the light of God's love and provision, were further revelation of His desire and power to work through us.

Just the week before I taught a lesson emphasizing God's purpose and plan for us regardless of our physical and mental capabilities. I recalled the prayer we said for the children, "Dear Lord, thank You for creating me and loving me just as I am. Thank You for having a plan for my life. Help me to do what You want me to." Although another person planted the seed of faith in Helen's heart some years before, the Lord was using me to cultivate the tender sprout so it would grow.

No other work—volunteer or otherwise—offers greater fulfillment than this. And it goes far beyond mere personal fulfillment. When, in the name of Jesus, you accept a challenge that involves the souls of the multiply-handicapped, you receive an abundance of special benefits. One benefit is a fuller measure of faith to share. Another is an ability to love that surpasses human design and motivation. Still another, and by far the greatest, is the presence of God's Spirit.

Yes, the Holy Spirit is the ultimate "benefit." When you contemplate the mental and physical hurdles a teacher must overcome to teach the handicapped spiritual truths, you realize it is not humanly possible. Only the Lord can overcome such obstacles. Only He can make Himself and His kingdom real to them. He uses man to speak His words and to express His love, but He alone enlightens. It was He who comforted Helen. It was He who provided her a purpose for living. And it was He who gave her that peace that passes all understanding.

My experiences with Helen and the other children have given me the answer to the inevitable question, "Can the retarded really comprehend abstract Bible truths and apply them to their lives?"

"Yes," I answer confidently, "by the grace of God they can!"

6

OH, HOLY NIGHT!

IT WAS DESERTED backstage. An eerie silence lurked in the shadows. The curtain hung like a giant, gloved hand muffling the sound of arriving guests. Before me stretched the electrical board—a sprawling mechanical monster with a 50-watt bulb its single sinister eye. The numerous plugs and switches seemed comparatively simple in the beginning. The closer it got to show time the more intricate looking they became. No doubt about it, as stage manager, key grip, and head curtain puller, I was feeling the weight of my responsibilities.

"It's going to be rough!" I groaned.

After the previous night's fiasco, I seriously doubted we could bring off this Christmas program. We came to the dress rehearsal with hopeful anticipation. Three hours later, confusion had us by the throat. Our biggest problem was the woman assigned to the spotlight. Having missed the previous rehearsals, she needed time, no longer available, to become proficient in her job. Unfortunately, my confinement to the stage made prompting her impossible. The spotlight was a portable one she would operate from the audience. Added to this concern was the fear the program's split-second timing was completely beyond us. And to top it all off, our only light backstage was the feeble glow from the electrical cyclops, plus a flashlight or two.

"Yes, Jane, it's going to be rough!" I repeated.

Suddenly bumping and straining sounds in the darkened stairwell announced the arrival of Millie's wheelchair. This meant the children were in the various assigned rooms being costumed and entertained until time for their appearance.

Across the stage a flashlight went on. Two ladies began setting up chairs for the children who would enter from that direction. I checked the props to make certain everything was ready. The wheelchair was in its proper place just out of sight of the audience. It would be my job to roll it to center stage at the precise moment.

As I mentally checked off the duties before me, a housefather arrived with Millie draped over his arms. Depositing her in the wheelchair, he gave her head a pat, and left. As I handed her the blanketed doll, she looked up at me with shining eyes. "Yes, Millie," I assured her, "the big night is finally here!"

Just then a shepherd, three flowers, a king, and Joseph clumped onto the stage and into my side of the wings. Helping them find their chairs, I noticed the ladies across the way doing the same with their children.

Enthusiastic applause suddenly penetrated the closed curtain. Dorothy was introducing the young man to give the welcoming speech. This was our first cue. The program had begun.

I grabbed the three flowers and arranged them on stage. From the other wings came four raindrops and a tree. When everyone was in place, I rushed to hit the houselights, then to the curtain, pulling it open in time for the spotlight. Counting ten seconds, I closed the curtain, helped the children off, and got ready for the next scene. Back I ran to the curtain, opening it in time again for the spotlight. Then counting ten seconds I pulled the curtain closed. It was amazing how smoothly things were going. Apparently my earlier concern was unfounded. The woman behind the spotlight was an instrument of precision and timing. For the next thirty minutes her movements and mine were perfectly synchronized.

Midway in the program one of the young men was scheduled to sing a solo from the risers in front of the stage. The curtain was open. The stage was dark. A simulated stained-glass window of colored cellophane stood in the center, with one of the smaller girls kneeling before it. A lamp was behind the cellophane. I was to flip the switch for a lovely silhouette effect when the number ended.

While the soloist sang the familiar hymn, I became so engrossed in his singing I didn't notice the little figure strolling out onto the stage. Timmy, a seven-year-old, was peering through the darkness into the audience. I saw him simultaneously with his call, "Mama!" Kicking off my shoes, I hurried out to retrieve him. Just as I encircled him from the back and hoisted him off the floor, we were hit by the full force of the spotlight! One . . . two . . . three . . . the seconds ticked by. I stood frozen, my mouth hanging open. Then blessed darkness. Swinging around I made my first graceful move towards the wings when on came the spotlight again. Apparently our precision instrument had developed a short.

Somehow I managed to gallop off behind the concealing fold of the curtain with Timmy dangling from one arm. The spot went off. The solo ended. The child was in place before the window. I flipped the switch, and the audience went "Ahhhhhhh!"

From that moment, everything went wrong. The curtain stuck. I hit the wrong switches. We missed cues. I had the desperate feeling our months of prayer and preparation were slipping down the drain. And all the while we were slipping and sinking, the program was building to a climax—the birth of our Lord. I checked Millie. She had the doll over her shoulder—upside down. It figures, I thought. Righting the baby, I stood poised for the final scene.

Then a soft blue light fell on center stage. The choir began singing "O Holy Night." "This is it, Millie!" I whispered as I gave the wheelchair a push to glide it into place. It didn't budge. I quickly checked to see what was blocking the wheels. Nothing. I pushed again, but the wheelchair remained stubbornly in its hidden corner. By now Joseph, the shepherds, and the kings were kneeling in a lonely semicircle on stage. Suddenly I saw it—the little lock and chain attached to the left wheel. The housefather, not wanting Millie to roll away, had innocently locked the wheels.

The singing ended leaving me clinging numbly to the wheelchair. The spotlight blinked off. I knew I had to move. I closed the curtain and hit the houselights. Pastor Stoddard came forward to give the benediction.

As he concluded, we began straightening up backstage. Millie didn't seem to realize she missed her big moment. I was grateful for that. When the housefather came to get her, I didn't have the heart to tell him what happened.

He left the stage with Millie gathered into his arms and me plodding down the stairs behind him. At the front of the hall three hundred guests were enjoying refreshments with the children still in costume. I wanted to slip out a side exit to avoid meeting anyone. But waiting for me at the foot of the stairs was my husband. His eyes were red. He had been crying.

"It wasn't *that* bad!" I said, fighting tears myself.

"Bad!" he exclaimed, his chin quivering at some tender memory. "It's the best Christmas program you've ever had!"

Then he asked a question that kept me awake for hours pondering the power of God's love. "And how in the world were you ever able to bring it off without a hitch?"

> *And we know that all things work*
> *together for good to them that*
> *love God, to them who are the*
> *called according to his purpose*
> *(Romans* 8: 28).

7

ONCE AROUND THE FLOOR
TO "FAITH OF OUR FATHERS"

THE CAR LURCHED along the dirt road from the highway to the school. The five of us bounced around like loose beads in a drawer as its wheels rolled over clods of dried mud and dipped into sunken tire tracks.

"Jane, did you tell the housemothers we're coming?" Sally asked above the chatter in the back seat.

"Yes," I replied, "they're expecing us."

We pulled into a clearing before six drab, box-like buildings. This day, the familiar sight of peeling paint, neglected grounds, and rusting play equipment failed to dampen our enthusiasm. We were bringing a surprise treat of cupcakes and punch, and we knew how happy the children would be.

As we began to unload, students appeared from everywhere—giggling, touching, peeking into the boxes; then running to tell others of our arrival. Within minutes grinning purple moustached people were licking crumbs and bits of frosting off sticky fingers.

When every morsel had been consumed and every drop drained, kids and volunteers tramped into the recreation room for a community sing. Sally slid onto the piano bench. Soon the room was reverberating from the force of her playing.

We had just launched into a chorus of "Bill Bailey"

when one of the children, a 45-year-old mongoloid, approached me with an invitation to dance. He was not much taller than my five feet, and the hand he offered was stubby and awkward. With his dentures in his pocket his smile had an irresistible impishness impossible to refuse. We struck out across the small room not quite in time with the beat. Other couples joined us. Laughter mingled with the music as we collided now and then on the crowded floor.

Something special happened that day. We were not just volunteers ministering to the social needs of the handicapped. We were ladies enjoying an hour of fun and fellowship with a group of friends.

The following week, I stood in the church parlor doorway waiting for the children to arrive. Sally pounded out a hymn on the piano with her usual dedication. Through the entrance appeared my dance partner of the week before. Suddenly he heard the music and saw me; the reflection of a memory burst brightly across his face. Before I could voice an objection, he caught me in a strong embrace and swept us into the room. We dipped and twirled around the flower bedecked altar to the toe-tapping strains of "Faith of Our Fathers." I could vaguely make out the ladies' astonished expressions as we pirouetted by.

Even if he is retarded he should know better, I thought as I pushed against him to disengage myself. He looked into my flushed and frowning face, his shoulders and head sagging. I was just about to scold him when a Psalm teased its way across my memory, "Let them praise His name with dancing. . . ."

That evening I shared the experience with my husband and two sons. Each laughed uproariously at his mental picture of mom and her partner cutting a fancy figure in the church parlor. But the laughter soon died away and we sat quietly for several minutes. In that silent communion, I sensed the Teacher tenderly leading us to a deeper understanding—each one receiving according to the needs of his heart.

8

THE LITTLE SHALL LEAD THEM

"I NEED TO TALK to you about Jeff," there was emotion and urgency in the housemother's voice.

Driving to the school in answer to her call, I thought back to the last time I saw the ten-year-old. He seemed his usual energetic self. But Mrs. Sullivan said to come as soon as possible. So, it must be something serious, I figured, as I pulled into the parking lot.

Walking up the ramp to the dorms, I found her waiting. "Thank you for coming, Mrs. Clark," she said almost apologetically.

"Not at all," I assured her. As we settled into overstuffed chairs, I asked, "Is something the matter with Jeff?"

"Well, nothing more than usual. What I really need to talk to you about concerns myself as well." She paused. When I didn't respond, she continued, "You see, Jeff being hyperactive is a handful for me. I've noticed that for several days after attending your worship service, he's so much better. I was wondering . . ."

This time I encouraged her, "Yes?"

"Well, do you think it would be all right if I prayed with him on the days between the services?"

It took several moments for her words to sink in. I had hurried here expecting something urgent. Now, it seemed, she merely wanted my approval to pray.

Suddenly her expression told me it *was* a serious matter. "I'm not a religious person, Mrs. Clark. I don't go to church," the words came quickly. "I believe in God, but frankly I've had little experience with Him. I know that something happens to Jeff when he's been in touch with God through your program. He's a happier, better adjusted person. Much easier to take care of, too. So, for his sake, as well as my own, I want him to have this sense of contentment throughout the entire week. I thought if he and I prayed together, it would help."

"Of course," I said.

"But are you *sure* it will be all right? I really don't know how to pray."

"God's not concerned with the words you use, Mrs. Sullivan. Or how polished you are at praying. It's the attitude of your heart—your sincerity—that's important to Him." Then I added, "The children are a perfect example of this."

A smile crept around the corners of her mouth. "I know," she sighed.

Driving home later, the prospect of God using Jeff to speak to Mrs. Sullivan generated a barrage of exciting thoughts. I could see them finding a place to themselves—perhaps by Jeff's bed, or in a corner of the multipurpose room. They would pray. Jeff would lead off in his enthusiastic way, followed by Mrs. Sullivan. Each day they would come together this way to pray. God would hear them and respond.

"Wow!" I said aloud.

Pulling up before the house, I remained in the car a while before joining the busy activity inside. In the quiet interlude, I prayed for this thoughtful woman who recognized God's positive effect on Jeff. And then I asked a special blessing on this retarded child whom the Lord had obviously chosen as His instrument for leading.

"God works in mysterious ways His wonders to perform!" I announced as I slammed the car door and hurried up the walk.

The wolf also shall dwell with the lamb, and the leopard shall lie down with the kid; and the calf and the young lion and the fatling together; and a little child shall lead them (Isaiah 11: 6).

9

GLAD TO BE GOD'S GUESTS

THE WOMAN'S VOICE sounded pleasant, friendly, and enthusiastic. Before he knew what was happening, the young minister agreed to meet her outside his church the following Wednesday.

Hmmmmm, he thought, this is the first time I've ever loaned my church to a stranger, and over the phone yet.

As they had talked, Mrs. Clark explained she headed a Christian education program for the mentally retarded. Her "students" were being housed temporarily at the state institution while their new residence-school was under construction in a nearby community.

"It's so cramped and noisy in the room we've been using," she explained, "it's difficult to achieve a worshipful atmosphere."

Her words had thrown him. His church was located on the grounds of the institution for the mentally ill. He knew that achieving anything worshipful was not just difficult but next to impossible! Many of his congregation had rational moments. But the retarded were different. Their handicap was constant. They had no moments of clear reasoning. So how could she expect them to achieve any semblance of worship, he wondered.

As he looked forward to Wednesday, he thought of it not as a spiritual experience, but as an exercise in Christian babysitting.

When he saw them waiting outside the church the following week, he was surprised. The group was larger than he expected. There were at least thirty people.

It was difficult to pick out Mrs. Clark. Almost everyone was waving and smiling. As he made his way up the walk to the door, a bird-like woman in a wheelchair grabbed his arm. He was shaken when she raised his hand to her lips and kissed it. At the same time a woman stepped from the group to greet him. "Hi, Reverend Black! I'm Dorothy Clark."

Nodding in reply, he unlocked the door and led the unlikely looking parade into the vestibule. As the children reacted noisily to the new surroundings, Mrs. Clark said firmly, "Remember, this is God's house. We are His guests."

With comparative control, they proceeded into the sanctuary and took places in the front pews. Flowers from someone's garden were arranged on the piano. Two candles, set in holders, decorated the choir loft railing. Collection baskets were removed from a grocery bag, and pennies were passed for the offering.

They've thought of everything, he had to admit.

Suddenly disbelief hit him like ice water in the face. One of the volunteers was asking the children, "Who would like to light the candles today?"

As if to soothe his jangled nerves, a grey-haired woman began playing the piano. A tall youth carefully struck a match, and under the tutelage of the volunteer, lit the candles. Slowly, Reverend Black relaxed.

"I was glad . . . " a woman recited. Immediately others joined in, ". . . when they said unto me, let us go into the house of the Lord."

Then, without direction, they stood. "Holy, holy, holy, Lord God almighty. . . ." As near as he could tell, almost everyone was singing.

He had taken a seat near the back so that he could slip out once the service began. But now he felt drawn to remain. There was something special about this group. He had to know what it was.

Watching the children closely, he began to understand.

These retarded people knew what they were doing—undoubtedly only by rote, but even so it was more than he expected.

Suddenly two stocky mongoloid men marched up the aisle. Uninvited, but apparently welcome, they stood before the group.

He gasped as they stretched out their arms to form human crosses.

A woman walked between them smiling. "I guess we can take a hint," she said. Then turning to the pianist, "Let's begin the sing time with 'The Old Rugged Cross.' " From the two men's expressions, she had read them correctly. They remained like statues during the entire hymn. Their solemn faces, with eyes raised heavenward, touched Black deeply.

The second and third songs, "Do Lord" and "Jesus Wants Me for a Sunbeam," contrasted sharply with the first. Accompanied by gestures and clapping, they provided joyful noises unto the Lord! Black got up from his remote position and moved closer to the front. When the children began the chorus of his favorite hymn, he found himself joining in, "And He walks with me, and He talks with me, and He tells me I am his own . . ."

Following the singing, the thank-you prayer time was announced. Again, without invitation, children walked to the front. A dark, heavy-set girl in her twenties began, "God, I have to go to the dentist. My tooth hurts. I love my housemother." Next, one of the human crosses stepped forward. Laying claim to Roy Rogers, Dale Evans, and Hoss and Little Joe Cartwright as his "cousins," he asked God's blessing on each one. "Take care of them, please," he concluded.

As the children prayed, Black observed their obvious trust in the One to whom they brought their petitions. They spoke with a sincerity that gave dignity to what otherwise might sound comical.

When the children returned to their seats, Mrs. Clark came to the front, her arms laden with materials. Black was caught up again with the others, this time in the lesson—a lesson that opened with the familiar experience of a picnic and moved steadily towards a single truth: God is the ultimate source of happiness.

It was a good lesson. But the exciting thing was the children. Hands waved eagerly to answer questions. And what they said revealed a spiritual understanding that surpassed mere learning by rote. These kids were reacting! They were involved! Oh, not all of them, of course. There were those whose thoughts were obviously detached from the present; others whose comprehension seemed limited to the love which permeated the sanctuary. But the responses of those who participated could mean only one thing.

With his heart pounding in his ears, Black felt the presence of God. And with this Presence came an undeniable call—an expansion of his ministry to the mentally retarded. It was settled.

As the activity around him slipped from his awareness, an exciting idea was born. Why not ask some of the patients in his congregation to work with him in his outreach to the retarded? What better therapy could there be for mind and soul, he reasoned, than helping those with greater problems than your own.

When the service ended he jumped to his feet. Midway up the aisle, he began calling, "Mrs. Clark! Mrs. Clark!"

Reaching her side, he pumped her hand vigorously. "They can understand," he cried, "they can *really* understand!"

> . . . *that their hearts may be encouraged as they are knit together in love, to have all the riches of assured understanding and the knowledge of God's mystery, of Christ . . . (Colossians 2: 2 RSV).*

10

A POTENTIAL FOR LOVELINESS

DOROTHY GLANCED at the faces in the audience turned in her direction. "Stop this silly trembling!" she scolded herself.

For weeks she had prayed about speaking at this women's association luncheon, but a feeling of dread persisted. What she had to say to these women would be difficult for them to hear, and it wasn't her nature to hurt intentionally. Her thoughts went back to an afternoon two months ago.

It all began in this same room. Instead of gaily decorated tables, there were rows of stiff folding chairs with thirty-five retarded children and adults seated restlessly. One of the children, Paula, was screaming and kicking convulsively. Although it was never determined what caused her frenzied actions, she was soon beyond control—her own or anyone else's. Reluctantly Dorothy motioned for two volunteers to take the girl from the room. They gathered Paula into their arms, crossed to the back and out the rear door.

Entering the corridor with the still jerking body between them, they collided with a group of women leaving a meeting across the hall. Although the volunteers were having great difficulty, not one of the women offered help. Instead they gingerly passed by, avoiding any eye or body contact with the swinging arms and legs. As they continued down the hall, one woman was heard to say disdainfully, "Why do they bring those people to church!"

"How I would love to tell her!" Dorothy said when told of the incident.

Although the congregation was generous in its financial support of the program the women in the hall were not the first to react negatively to the retarded. Fear and misconception kept many from actual contact with the children. An overwhelming sense of pity rendered others incapable of helping. And to be honest, there was something deeper than pity or fear that caused still others to avoid involvement. It was undoubtedly this feeling of revulsion—aroused by Paula's violent thrashing—that motivated the woman in the corridor to question the retarded's place in church. Later, when asked to speak before the women's association, it was clear to Dorothy what her topic would be.

". . . and Dorothy is here to tell us of her interesting work," a friendly voice was saying.

Hearing her name, Dorothy snapped back to the present. As she stood, rustling and murmuring skipped along the tables. When the room was quiet she began, "Someone from this group asked a question recently, and I am here to answer it."

Without further comment, she picked up a rose and began tearing off the petals, one by one. Holding up the flower, she spoke, "God created this flower. It is now mutilated and ugly. Nevertheless, it is His creation. He created it with the potential for loveliness as He creates all life. We would throw away this rose. There would be no place for such a flower in our bouquet."

Tossing the rose to the floor, Dorothy continued, "We might compare the mentally and physically handicapped to this flower. God created them, also. They, too, are damaged and often difficult to look upon. Nevertheless, they are His creation. He created them with the potential for loveliness."

She paused, clasping her hands. "What do we do with the mentally retarded? Do we cast them aside like our

49

rose? Do we say, 'There's no place for them in *my* life—in *my* church'?"

The room was suspended in silence. Every eye was locked on her.

"Genesis 1: 26 says that man is created in God's image. Does this verse relate only to the beautiful and intelligent, or is the essence of God's character within each human being regardless of his appearance and mental capacity?"

To answer her own question, Dorothy spoke of six-year-old Susie, and her simple trust in Jesus as her friend; of Ruth who radiates joy although she is bound in a silent world to her wheelchair; and of Helen, who in turning to God learned to accept herself in the light of His love and provision.

"As I have been working with the retarded," Dorothy continued, "I have found there is a soul within each one no matter how severe the handicap—a lovely potential waiting to be discovered. When that inner spirit is exposed to God's love, it blossoms, responds, and grows stronger. A life that is lonely, like Susie's, painful, like Ruth's, and frustrated, like Helen's, becomes one of purpose and hope. You and I can't accomplish this—only the Lord can. But He needs our hearts and hands to use as His own. This," she emphasized, "is why we bring the retarded to church—to be loved, comforted, and taught in the name of Jesus."

The room was heavy with emotion. "There are physically and mentally handicapped people who have never heard of our loving Heavenly Father," Dorothy went on. "For one reason or another they have been spiritually written off—condemned to a life void of the joy and hope only our resurrected Lord can inspire. No one tells them that God loves them just as they are; that they can call on Him in prayer and He will answer. But God does love them. He will respond to their petitions.

"The retarded need God. God needs us. As Paul puts it in his letter to the Corinthians, 'So now then we are ambassadors for Christ . . .' We have a unique opportunity here in our church to be ambassadors to the retarded. Each week 30 to 35 children come for a special worship service. We average only six volunteers. We need at least two or three times that number to give the children the love and attention they deserve."

Drawing in a deep breath, Dorothy began her final remarks, "I came here today to answer a question posed by one of you regarding the retarded's place in church. Now I ask you: Do you believe there is a place for the retarded in your church? If so, could you put aside pity, fear, and revulsion, and share with them the love that God abundantly supplies? If your answer is Yes then the 'least of these' ask you to share your faith with them."

Dorothy looked into the faces. Many were tear-streaked. All showed the impact of her words. "Will you help?" she asked.

Although her hands still trembled, Dorothy felt peace within as she sank into her chair. The difficult task was over. Now it was up to the Lord.

And now, Lord, what wait I for?
my hope is in thee (*Psalm* 39: 7).

WEBSTER DEFINES hope as "a feeling that what is wanted will happen." But can one, whose mind will never develop beyond the level of a child's, hope for that which is realistic?

Elizabeth, a young mongoloid, is obsessed with becoming a bride and mother. She constantly asks for magazines featuring bridal gowns and paraphernalia, and draws touching stick-figure mothers carrying stick-figure babies in their stomachs. No, hope for the retarded goes beyond "a feeling that what is wanted will happen."

For the retarded, hope is knowing there is meaning and purpose to their lives—that God loves them as they are—and that someday they will be with the Lord, trapped no longer in their imperfect, human bodies. A woman who had been struggling with the crushing realization that she was "different," shared what the Lord had done for her. "I've been troubled about the way I am," she said. "I've given it to the Lord and He is giving me a real peace about it. He is helping me to accept myself as I am." Peace—acceptance of self—dependence on God—this is hope.

To you who face the responsibility of caring for a retarded loved one, it may seem impossible that he could ever comprehend God's love and provision for him. But nowhere in Scripture does it say that the hope of the Gospel message is for the normal only. Hope is a delicate gift which the retarded need your help to unwrap.

11

BEND DOWN TO GOD'S LEVEL

APPLAUSE FILLED the large dining hall as Dorothy maneuvered her way through the crowded room to her table. Although she was grateful the demonstration of her teaching methods had gone well, the prospect of speaking before the hundred or so conference members had caused nervous flutterings which even now refused to subside.

The woman seated next to her was wiping away tears.

"He could understand that!" she exclaimed. "He *could* understand that!"

As she continued to dab at her eyes, her story came tumbling out. Her parents had taken a foster child into their home. He was retarded. The family often told the boy that God loved him.

"But not until I heard you speak tonight did I realize that he could love God in return." For a moment she was unable to continue. "It never occurred to me that he could understand that Jesus was his friend—someone he could talk to, depend on, fellowship with, claim for his own. But when you spoke of using common, familiar objects to demonstrate Bible truths, I suddenly realized that Tom could have understood."

Dorothy smiled reassuringly. "It's never too late to begin teaching him," she said.

"I know," replied the woman, "but he's no longer with us. Several years ago it was decided he should be placed in a state institution. I'm sorry that while he was with us I never helped him to find contentment in the Lord."

Moved by the woman's obvious dejection, Dorothy offered to go with her to visit Tom.

"But what could we do?" the woman asked.

"We could take a picnic lunch and sit on the grass and talk," Dorothy began. "I have a balsa wood airplane Tom could play with. I've used it to help the children see that although we may not understand how an airplane works, we can still take a ride on one—and even if we can't understand all there is to know about God, we can still accept His love and love Him in return. Tom can't understand spiritual truths at our level, so it's necessary to bend down to his level. And if we begin with something he is already familiar with—like the airplane—it will be easier for him to grasp something new."

The woman was grateful for Dorothy's offer and took her telephone number to arrange a definite date later.

Alone in her room that night, Dorothy kept remembering the woman's poignant confession.

"I wonder how many have made the same mistake," she thought, "limiting God's power because a mind is suspended in some stage of childhood. If they could only realize it's that very simplicity, the child-likeness, that reaches out so longingly to God."

In the months ahead waiting for the woman to call, Dorothy would often look back to their conversation that evening and wonder about Tom. She had known so many like him—young people frustrated by minds struggling against boundaries set by retardation, and lonely in bodies reaching for potentials never fulfilled.

"Only the Lord can give meaning to a life such as Tom's," Dorothy thought.

But who would help him to know Jesus as his personal friend and Savior? Would anyone even try?

How then shall they call on him in whom they have not believed? and how shall they believe in him of whom they have not heard? (Romans 10: 14.)

12

THIS LITTLE PIGGY WENT TO MARKET

HE WALKED DOWN THE AISLE pushing the loaded shopping cart before him. As he neared the checkout counter, he made certain there was no one of authority near. The plump young woman was alone behind the counter. Her small hands sorted, removed tags, added up figures, and bagged the merchandise. As she worked, his eyes glanced over the prominent signs announcing that for the next three days adult students of the local school for the retarded would be clerking in the thrift shop— an item which received wide publicity in the community newspapers.

It was a slow, plodding procedure but at last the packages were ready and the bill completed. He looked around again, then slipped her some play money.

"I can't accept this," she said.

"Why not?"

"Because it's not real money."

The man looked startled, then embarrassed. As he fumbled in his pocket, the woman's voice grew bolder.

"I may be retarded—but I'm not stupid!" she proclaimed. Each word was like a fist against his conscience.

He nervously pulled several dollars from his wallet, quickly gathered up his purchases and made for the door. The little figure stood silently looking after him.

It had taken her many frustrating years to understand that she was different. Along the difficult way she found the means to accept herself as she is.

"The Lord," she once shared, "has given me a peace about myself."

Could the man look at himself with such honesty and be at peace?

> *Peace is my parting gift to you, my own peace, such as the world cannot give. Set your troubled hearts at rest, and banish your fears (John 14: 27 NEB).*

13

NOT AGAIN!

RUTH WAS STRUGGLING against the relentless embrace of the wheelchair. Soft grunting sounds were audible evidence she was fighting hard to find a more comfortable position. Her small bony hands clutching the sides, reminded me of a baby bird hanging onto the nest at solo time. Slowly the struggling ceased, and her thin crippled body slipped resignedly downward until chin was locked against shallow bosom. As I approached she looked up as if to say, "I'm not surrendering, Dorothy— just resting between rounds."

There was no sign of resentment or self-pity in Ruth's actions. Toughened by fifty-six years of combat on the battlefield of the handicapped, she is above such human weakness. Although mentally and physically a loser by normal standards, she has a spirit which refuses to accept defeat! This inner strength, coupled with a gentle sense of humor, has armed her sufficiently to win at least a stand-off with the unknown enemy who attacked her before birth.

It was Wednesday afternoon and we were in the midst of our special worship service. The cavernous church hall, cold and impersonal before our arrival, was now warmed by the friction of noise and activity rubbed vigorously together.

As I lifted Ruth into a sitting position, I gave her a loving pat. Her lined face brightened with a smile of gratitude. Once upright again, she busily smoothed her rumpled skirt, then made a quick inspection of the two hearing aids tucked behind her ears—her fingers nimbly running down the insulated wires to the twin controls pinned to her chest. All was well. Her infant-like sounds communicated feeling rather than reason. She was delighted to be in church and wanted everyone to know it!

Chairs began to creak as anticipation erupted into an epidemic of the wiggles. It was "happy sing time," a rare moment when everyone, regardless of his limitations, could participate, share, and enjoy. We turned eagerly toward the piano, but in the unexpected absence of the pianist, it appeared mute and forlorn.

I wondered, will the kids be able to sing a cappella? Or should I proceed to the closing prayer time?

Not wanting to disappoint them, I decided to take a giant step in faith. "Children," I said, "we'll have to sing our hymns without the piano today. You know the songs so well I'm sure you'll have no trouble."

Humming the pitch, I began to encourage them along the first stanza. It was immediately apparent there would be no musical miracle that day as thirty-five voices bravely struggled off in thirty-five-part harmony!

Once in motion, it was impossible to stop. As it continued the discord grew worse, the children trying to correct their differences with raw volume. As the singing reached an awesome crescendo, it was Ruth who was first to react to the sour notes reverberating with stereophonic effect through her two hearing aids. With the aplomb of a seasoned technician she deftly adjusted the dials on the instrument panel across her chest. Then as if to make doubly sure she raised her hands and cupped them over her ears. Wrinkling her brow in despair, she shook her head in time with the music.

As the children became aware of the antics of the self-styled music critic, their singing came to a grinding halt—reminiscent of a Gramophone in desperate need of a rewind. Captivated, they watched Ruth twisting to and fro. Finally the spell was broken as a sprinkling of giggles gaily wafted upward, merging and swelling into a landslide of laughter.

The service ended abruptly with the benediction coming unexpectedly from the back row.

"Well," a booming voice called approvingly, "Ruth's done it again!"

She had "done it again" all right, and as long as the Lord keeps breathing life into her body she will continue doing it. Ruth has found purpose in her existence. She has claimed the joy that God creates within each person, and her special gift is the ability to share this joy with others.

> *Dear brothers, is your life full of difficulties and temptations? Then be happy, for when the way is rough, your patience has a chance to grow. So let it grow, and don't try to squirm out of your problems. For when your patience is finally in full bloom, then you will be ready for anything, strong in character, full and complete*
> *(James 1: 2-4 TLB).*

14

IT'S WHAT'S UP FRONT THAT COUNTS

"St-stu-stupid! Du-du-dumb!" Molly boomed in a strong directorial voice. "Th-the boys b-back th-there are t-tr-trees! Du-du-dumb!"

Just what our Christmas program needs, I thought. Another director.

Something was obviously bothering Molly about the boys in the back row, but exactly what was anybody's guess. Firm hands assisted the twenty-five-year-old woman to a chair as she continued giving directions. Whatever her problem, there was no time to resolve it now—not with thirty-five others eagerly demanding attention.

"Du-dumb t-tr-trees . . ." the barely discernible words continued to come. Suddenly from across the room an exasperated boy yelled, "Oh, shut up, Molly!" To everyone's amazement, Molly's mouth slowly closed. Instantly her hand darted upwards to find that favorite lock of hair—twist, turn, twist. . . .

As I watched the familiar procedure, I recalled how comparatively simple past programs had been before Molly joined the group. Her incorrigible behavior not only lengthened rehearsals and made them more difficult but it also challenged the very goals of the program.

Goals? I wasn't even certain what they were anymore. And were any goals worth this agony of preparation—the months of frustration, exhaustion, and tension—which culminated in one brief hour on stage? I knew the answer to that question lay in the overwhelming feeling of success and pride which the children experienced as a result of one brief hour in the spotlight. Yes, they needed this opportunity to be productive, to participate. How else could they find self-dignity in their limited life experience?

"So, the show must go on," I groaned.

Pinning color codes to the children's clothes to distinguish shepherds from kings, kings from trees, and trees from wisemen, the children were shown their places on stage. Matching colors were taped to the floor to help them remember where to stand.

"In th-the ba-back . . ." There she went again! This time Molly was standing close behind me. I could feel her heavy breathing coming in puffs and snorts through her deformed mouth and nose. A hairlip made her speech impossible to understand much of the time. The stuttering, fortunately, was not always present as it was today, brought on by the excitement of the rehearsal. As a volunteer encouraged her back to her chair, up went her hand again to twist and turn the lock of hair.

Taking advantage of the momentary quiet, I placed the cartoon charts against an easel. When there are only six to eight students who can read, special methods of teaching must be devised. Using pictures, whenever possible, to depict words is one way. A pattern of failure is broken for many children as they "read" the cartoons and learn a new song.

Voices were singing lustily when suddenly I felt like my left arm was being separated from my body. Next to hollering, this was Molly's favorite means of getting someone's attention. I loosened her grip. "Do-dor-dorothy . . ." she began. That did it. Although we had fifteen minutes left of rehearsal time, I excused the kids and volunteers, then collapsed into the nearest chair.

As I watched the children leave the multipurpose room to return to their dorms, more excited and happy than they'd been since this time last year, I had to admit I was enjoying it all myself—in spite of Molly. Over the years, some of our wildest and most meaningful experiences occurred in connection with the Christmas program. Undoubtedly, this year would be no different. Parents, too, looked forward to this time when their kids, so often pushed to the back and out of sight by the normal world, would be "stars" for a night.

I looked at my watch. Miss Burke, one of the school's teachers, was to meet with me before I left that afternoon. Earlier, she volunteered to select the child who could best handle the important role of narrator. Gratefully, I accepted her offer—one less detail for me to worry about. Now, she had made a selection. She, the student, and I were to have a private audition.

"Hi!" Miss Burke called as she entered the room. Striding behind her was the short, stocky form of Molly! I was speechless.

"I know what you're thinking," Miss Burke said with a smile, "but Molly does read well. She's been working very hard practicing with a tape recorder."

As I shook my head in disbelief, Miss Burke turned to Molly. "Read for Dorothy," she ordered calmly.

Molly pulled a chair close to mine. I saw a quieter, more controlled young woman than I'd seen before. She means business, I had to admit.

Molly began reading slowly, savoring every word. In spite of her severe speech impediment, I could understand her perfectly. When she finished, she closed the book and grabbed for her lock of hair. Restraint gone, she struggled for control. Words caught in her throat, "I-I-I read w-well!"

"Yes, you do, Molly," I agreed. "The part is yours."

The next two weeks were a haze of activity. Finally the night of the program arrived. Three hundred chairs were set up in the Fellowship Hall for the many friends and relatives—some family members coming from other states. The risers for the choir were to the left of the stage on the main floor. There in dead center in front of everything and everyone were two chairs and a mike for Molly and me.

Shortly before eight, we all took our places. The house-lights dimmed. Seated next to me, Molly reached for her hair, then let her hands fall gracefully into her lap. "Thanks, Lord," I sighed. Molly's parents had been pointed out to me earlier. I could see them watching her every move from the second row.

I walked to the microphone. "We pray you will receive this program with the same measure of love with which it is given," was my brief greeting.

As I returned to my seat, the music swelled, then softened. Gently I touched Molly. She rose and walked to the microphone.

Slowly and distinctly she began to read from the Gospel of Luke. These were not mere words she spoke. Molly was sharing the excitement and joy of the birth of Christ. To her, it was no fairy tale. She was reading of a Christ she knows—a person who comforts her when people like myself are too busy to try to understand her. Sensing this, the audience listened spellbound.

That night we began the program with the climax. Immediately following the final curtain, Molly's mother rushed forward. Although I had never met the woman before, she embraced me warmly.

"You just can't realize what you've done for our daughter," she began. "Although Molly is quite capable, she has always been put in the back. But not tonight!"

Suddenly everything became clear. Molly's previous preoccupation with the back row was not out of concern for the children there. She had been afraid of being stuck in the back herself. So, she ridiculed the boys, "Du-du-dumb t-t-trees," hoping to avoid joining them.

How simple, yet intense, was Molly's need to be up front—to be accepted—to be recognized as a person. And the One who is infinitely wise saw both her need and her potential. I knew, without doubt, Molly's big moment was all His doing.

Thank you, God, I breathed deeply, and went to greet the other guests.

For he hath not despised nor abhorred the affliction of the afflicted; neither hath he hid his face from him; but when he cried unto him, he heard (Psalm 22: 24).

15

THIS OLD HOUSE

ON THE DAY FOLLOWING her mother's funeral, Dorothy stopped by the church to check her box in the Christian education office. There in a neat, but now pathetic, pile were seven get-well cards for her mother. Each was individually drawn and lettered. Each bore the distinctive mark of its creator. As Dorothy read the simple sentiments, tears came once again.

Later, at home, she put the cards in a drawer for safe keeping. Somehow she must explain her mother's death to the children in the light of their prayers for her recovery.

"Oh, Lord," she whispered, "it's hard for me to accept and understand. How can I explain it so they will understand?"

Two days later she walked into the classroom with what she knew was the explanation God had provided.

As she sketched a house on the blackboard, complete with chimney, curtains at the windows, and shingles on the roof, her hands trembled. The prospect of discussing her mother's death kept the deep wound of sorrow open.

"Hi, Dorothy! . . . Hey, Dorothy, I'm here! . . . Dorothy!" Suddenly the children's greetings preceded them into the room. And they came tumbling after.

For the next fifteen minutes, volunteers welcomed the children, completed preparations for the service, and conducted the opening ceremonies. Then it was time for the lesson.

As she walked forward, Dorothy prayed silently, "Lord, help me not to break down, not to break down, not to break down . . ." Turning to face the children, she said, "I have something important to tell you. The prayers you have been saying for my mother have been answered." Her words caused a ripple of nodding heads. "But," she went on, "not in the way you expected. Just six days ago, the Lord took my mother home to be with Him."

As she paused, several of the more sensitive children began to cry.

"Thank you for your prayers," Dorothy continued, "and for the beautiful cards you made for her. I loved my mother deeply. I'm going to miss her very much." She held up her Bible. "We found my mother's Bible by her bedside, open. One of the last things she did before she died was read the Scriptures. My mother loved the Lord. She is with Him now. This is a great comfort to me."

The composure and confidence with which she spoke, had a soothing effect on the children. Eyes were dried and noses blown. When the room was quiet, Dorothy walked to the blackboard. Her fingers gripped the cool surface of the chalk. All at once she heard a soft whisper, "But why, Dorothy? Why did your mother die?"

"We're going to talk about that," she answered, "right now. Children, the part of my mother that felt and gave love, that laughed and was happy, that cried and was sad; the part that cared about others, her inner self—that part is not dead. Only her tired, sick body is dead."

Pointing to the house on the blackboard, Dorothy explained, "Our bodies are like houses—houses in which our inner selves live." With the chalk she made scribbling marks on the panes of a window.

"What happens when a windowpane is broken at school?" she asked.

"They fix it!" someone answered.

"Right," Dorothy encouraged, "and what if a few shingles are blown off and the roof begins to leak?" She made more scribbling marks on the roof.

Again the answer came, "Put more shingles on!"

"And when things go wrong with our bodies, like a sprained ankle, or a bad cold, or an earache, what do we do?"

"Go see the nurse!"

"Yes, we go to the nurse or doctor and they fix us." Turning back to her drawing, she continued, "Sometimes there is damage to a house that can't be fixed—like a flood comes and causes cracks in the foundation. Or perhaps a house becomes so old it just wears out—like a pair of old tennies." Additional scribbling marks were drawn across the foundation and other parts of the house. "When a house is too damaged or too old to be fixed, what must we do?"

"You have to get another house."

"Move."

"Stay in a motel."

"Yes," Dorothy agreed, "we must find a better house in which to live. And when our bodies get too old or are too sick to be fixed, God gives us a new body to live in. This is what happened to my mother. Her body, the house her inner self lived in, couldn't be fixed. It was too sick. So God prepared a new, strong, perfect body for her in Heaven. When my mother left her old body, she went to Heaven in a brand new body that will never, never, never wear out or have anything wrong with it. This is what we can all look forward to as members of God's family."

Putting down the chalk, Dorothy walked over to stand before the children. "Our present bodies—our houses for our inner selves—may have something wrong with them, like weak eyes or ears, or a stiff leg or arm, but when God gives us our new bodies, they will be perfect. No shingles will be missing from our roofs. Our foundations won't crumble," as she spoke, the children began to laugh and relax, "and our windows won't be broken."

Picking up her Bible again, she opened to John 14: 1. "These words I will read were spoken by Jesus to comfort His disciples. He was about to die on the cross and go to Heaven. His disciples wouldn't be seeing Him for awhile. Jesus knew they would miss Him—as I miss my mother. Jesus told them not to worry. His words are meant for us, too. Listen. 'Let not your heart be troubled: ye believe in God, believe also in me. In my Father's house are many mansions: if it were not so, I would have told you. I go to prepare a place for you. And if I go and prepare a place for you, I will come again, and receive you unto myself; that where I am, there ye may be also.' Children, Jesus has prepared a place for each of us in Heaven. Knowing this, we don't have to fear death, for ourselves or those we love. When God wants us to come home to Him, we merely pack up all of our good possessions—joy, love, peace, compassion— and leave all of the bad things behind—pain, loneliness, sickness, sorrow." As she concluded, Dorothy patted herself, "Someday I'll be through with this old house. Then I'll move into the new house God has prepared for me!"

Later that evening, Dorothy reread the cards the children made for her mother. This time there were no tears.

"Help me, Lord," she prayed, "to commend this one I loved so dearly to You—with no strings of agony or remorse attached. And thank You, Lord," she added, "not only for what You inspired me to share with the children, but for what You gave to me through my giving to them."

> *But our commonwealth is in heaven, and from it we await a Savior, the Lord Jesus Christ, who will change our lowly body to be like his glorious body, by the power which enables him even to subject all things to himself*
> *(Philippians 3: 20, 21 RSV).*

16

FROM THE MOUTHS OF BABES

"Who helps us when we have a problem?"

"Jesus!"

"How do we ask Jesus to help us?"

"Pray!"

I was seated near the back of the room watching Dorothy interact with the class. Carrying a mixed bouquet, she walked down the aisle encouraging different ones to touch and smell the blossoms. Taking the hand of a blind boy, she guided it over the petals of a rose. Then brushing his fingers along the stem, she explained, "Those sharp things are thorns, Hal."

Turning her attention to the class, she asked, "Because there are things about this flower that aren't so beautiful, should we throw it away?"

"No" was the popular reply.

Then arranging the bouquet in a vase, she likened people to the flowers—all different, yet each one beautiful in his own way. Selecting a daisy, she looked around the room. "I might have something wrong with me— like this flower might have something wrong with it." As Dorothy spoke, she pulled a petal from the daisy. "Perhaps you have a problem, too," a second then third petal fell to the table, "like an arm or leg that doesn't work. Or maybe you can't read, or it's hard for you to talk. But God loves us just as we are." By now five or six petals lay scattered on the table.

Across the aisle from me six-year-old Susie sat teetering in her chair. When Dorothy began plucking at the flower, Susie's eyes widened and her mouth drooped downward. Suddenly, she scurried up the aisle.

The room was still as the tiny figure gathered up the petals one by one. Cupping them in her hands, she offered Dorothy the bits of flower.

As Dorothy reached to receive her offering, Susie summarized the lesson in one brief statement, "It's all right—Jesus will fix it!"

As she bounced back to her seat, I surveyed the room. There were many things that needed fixing—twisted bodies, mute tongues, deaf ears, blind eyes, and retarded minds. Each child represented a depth of heartache inconceivable to families with normal children.

I thought of my own little niece. "Hey, Jane," my brother-in-law shouted over the phone, "It's a girl!" Three months later the diagnosis came—permanent brain damage.

How easy to turn from God in such tragedy—to question the reconcilability of a compassionate God with malformed babies. Yet, God does not turn from the handicapped. He is more concerned for them than the fallen sparrow; He numbers the hairs of their heads, also. Yes, God loves them, every one.

How do I know this? Susie told me . . . and David . . . and Molly . . . and Ruth . . . and Jim . . . and Millie . . . and Paula . . . and Doreen . . . .

> *Are not two sparrows sold for a penny? And not one of them will fall to the ground without your Father's will. But even the hairs of your head are all numbered. Fear not, therefore; you are of more value than many sparrows*
> *(Matthew 10: 29-31 RSV).*

17

THE DECISION

"Junior! Hey, Junior!" my brother's call bounced up the stairs ahead of his short legs and lively feet, "who's going away?"

Stepping outside my door, I tried to hush him, "Quiet, Jimmy! You want Mom to hear you?"

"I already tried asking her," his voice persisted loudly, "she just cried more." Then skidding to a halt before me, he puffed, "What's happening?"

"For an eight-year-old kid, you're not very smart!" I accused. Grabbing his arm, I hurried him into my room. "Come on in, Jim, and we'll talk."

As Jimmy thrust himself into my bean bag chair, a grin spread from ear to ear. He was never allowed to enter my room and rarely was he invited in. The novelty of being there so delighted him, he forgot, momentarily, the reason for his hasty arrival.

As his puzzled expression slowly returned, I knew it was time to begin, "Jimmy, Sis is growing up. She was twelve last week. It's been real hard for Mom and Dad with me away at college. When I was in high school I took care of Shelly while Mom shopped and ran errands. But for the past three years, there's been no one to leave her with. So, Mom and Dad have been thinking of sending Shelly to a school . . ."

"Shelly already goes to school!" Jimmy interrupted.

"I mean, to a school to live," I explained.

Jimmy's chin quivered. "They can't do that," his voice cracked, "I love Sis!"

Ruffling his hair, I tried to console my little brother, "I know you love her—we all do. Mom and Dad love her the most of anybody. But, Jimmy, sometimes the best decision is the hardest."

Flying out of the chair, Jimmy agonized, "How can 'best' be to send someone you love away? Just tell me that—tell me—go on!"

Dragging him over to my bed, I plopped down beside him. "Take it easy, Jimmy. You and I can never fully understand how it's been for Mom and Dad. When Sis was born, I was older than you are now. I remember what a pretty baby she was. She wasn't sick. But as she grew she didn't do the things other babies do. It was a long time before she could sit up. Mom had real trouble feeding her. We were afraid she would never walk."

"Oh, Junior," the voice interrupted again, "she walks good now. Even talks more than she used to. She knows a few of the words in my reader. And she can count to twenty. We have lots of fun. Sis understands almost everything you tell her. She just doesn't remember things."

"You're right, Jimmy," I encouraged, "Shelly can read a little, and she has learned to count to twenty. We all love her. She's a beautiful person. But how we feel about her is not what's most important. How Shelly feels about herself—that's the important thing." I put my arm about Jimmy's shoulders and hugged him to me. "If going away to school will help her be less afraid of people; will help her make friends; will help her discover there are all sorts of things she can do—then it's necessary she be given that chance. Not just so we can be proud of what she learns to do, but so she can be proud of herself! Do you see? It's for Shelly's own good."

"But," Jimmy continued his rebuttal, "Wayne has a cousin who's sorta like Shelly and his folks keep him at home."

"Each person is different, Jimmy. And each family situation is different, too. Some kids are better off remaining at home. But, we feel, it's better for Shelly to be with others like herself; to be cared for by people trained to help her reach her full potential—what she's capable of learning. Fortunately, Dad can afford to send her to this really neat school. Some families aren't so fortunate."

Jimmy's skinny frame rose and fell with a deep sigh. Propelling him towards the door, I said, "We'll all talk it over together before she leaves. Try to think of ways to help, okay, Jim?" He nodded as I booted him out the door, "Scram now kid—I've got studying to do!"

As Jimmy descended the stairs, he was a quieter, more thoughtful young man than the one who had bounded up them two at a time. I watched until he disappeared into the stairwell. Then closing my door, I looked around. Books lay scattered everywhere. As I straightened up the room, I thought of all the things I couldn't tell my little brother—how unhappy Mom and Dad were when they realized Sis was retarded. Mom cried and Dad yelled; each one thinking it was somehow his fault—blaming himself for something that happened or didn't happen. Both vowed there would be no more children. Then four years later, along came Jimmy.

As he and Shelly played happily together, Jimmy proved to be a blessing in disguise. Shelly actually improved. She learned so much from Jim. For awhile, their abilities were comparable, even with the difference in their ages. But now Jimmy was passing Shelly by. And the critical thing was Shelly knew it. She had gradually come to an awareness of how she really was, that she was incapable of doing most things for herself.

Part of her inability was the family's fault. We were all guilty of doing too much for her. And each time we stepped in and did what she could do for herself, we were saying in effect, you don't do it well enough, or fast enough. Unintentionally, we were robbing her of her sense of self-worth and dignity. When we realized what was happening we were even more concerned for Shelly.

As I looked down at the small impression of Jimmy's body in the bean bag chair, I recalled my conversation with the folks the summer before. "Shelly's very dependent on Mom and me," Dad said, a worried expression etched upon his face. "We're fearful of how she would get along should something suddenly happen to us—to either of us, for that matter. We've made inquiries at a school for the retarded and are impressed with the facilities and the around-the-clock professional care offered." I remembered the long, searching look which passed between them at this point. "So," Dad continued, "we've made a difficult and, we pray, wise decision—we've put Shelly's name on their waiting list. We feel timing is extremely important. Right now, Mom and I are healthy and strong—we could manage to keep her at home indefinitely. But, if something did happen and Shelly were placed somewhere under tragic circumstances, it would be a much greater adjustment for her to make. On the other hand, if she enters the school while we are still around, we can love her, encourage her, visit her, and have her home for visits. Yes," Dad concluded, "it's the best way, for Shelly's sake."

The call from the school came almost one year to the day later. "You may enroll Shelly," the voice said over the phone, "as soon as it is convenient for you." September first was agreed upon as her check-in date. And September first was just two weeks away.

Finishing my housekeeping chores, I picked up an economics book and stretched out on the bed. Before I began to study, I prayed that the next several months would pass quickly for us. We were in for a time similar to mourning, I was certain.

Well, the next three days, at least, slipped by almost unnoticed. Shelly returned from a visit to Gram's, where the folks sent her while they were making final arrangements with the school. Her first evening back, we had a family conference. It was Dad who told Shelly about the school. When she responded, "I won't go," we all put in an encouraging word. We stressed the new friends bit, the swimming pool; even enticed her with the pottery shop, the school's latest addition.

But it wasn't until Jimmy spoke up that we saw a glimmer of acceptance in Shelly. In his best voice-of-experience manner, he told her of his first trip to summer camp. "I was a little scared and lonesome at first," he admitted, "but that kinda stuff was over in a day or so. Then it was fun!"

Shelly straightened in her chair. She looked intently at her younger brother. Then she nodded. It was as if she were saying, "Well, if Jimmy can go away, so can I!"

The days continued to pass quickly. Mom spent the time sewing for Shelly. Jimmy fixed a photo album with Shelly's favorite snaps of the family. Dad made her a lovely wooden treasure box with a tiny lock and key. Yes, the days were busy and seemingly carefree. But at night the light stayed on in Mom and Dad's room until very late. Sometimes I heard Dad trying to reassure Mom they were doing the best thing for Shelly. Several times I thought they would cancel out before the first of September arrived.

And then it did arrive. With her treasures packed in a new suitcase, Shelly came downstairs to her last breakfast as a resident member of the family. Although we tried to make it a festive affair, the atmosphere was reminiscent of a condemned man's last meal. Mom talked too fast and too much, her habit when upset. Dad was quiet. Jimmy bolted his food and promptly got sick. I couldn't eat at all.

Because of his troubled tummy, Jimmy was to remain at home, and I was delegated to stay with him. Before the folks took Shelly to the school, I gave her a hug and fastened a copper cross around her neck. Into her purse I slipped a small New Testament. She smiled, waved, and walked out the front door. Then she was gone.

Within an hour, Mom and Dad were back home. The school was but a short distance away. Mom was tense as she explained we could not see Shelly for one month. One month! The school officials explained this was necessary to give Shelly time to adjust and begin to identify with her new surroundings.

"How did she take it?" I had to know.

Mom didn't reply; just hurried upstairs to her room. It was Dad who answered, "Fine—she took it just fine. Better than we did."

The next month was rough. Back in college, I found myself wanting to call the school to give the housemother a helpful hint or two on how to care for my sister.

And if I was reacting this way, I thought, what must Mom and Dad be going through?

The second week after Shelly's departure, I was home for the weekend. Mom talked constantly about bringing Shelly back. Then one night she completely fell apart.

"I'm going to get her," she shouted, "right now!"

Dad was great. He comforted Mom, but wouldn't let her rush off after Shelly, knowing that whatever good had been accomplished would be jeopardized by my frantic, lonely, well-meaning mother.

"The reasons for Shelly being there haven't changed, Honey," he said. "They never will."

Although there would be many more tears, that evening Mom finally accepted that Shelly no longer lived at home.

When the month was up, we made arrangements to see Sis. I came home from college so we could all be together for our first visit. I'll never forget that short drive to the school. It seemed endless. At last we pulled into the parking lot. Several children were waiting inside the entrance. Shelly was not one of them.

Walking towards the main building, we spotted her talking with a young girl. She saw us and waved for us to join them. How Dad beamed when Shelly introduced us to her friend.

Then, grabbing Jimmy's hand, she rushed him off toward the playground, with the rest of us trailing behind. After playing on the equipment, Sis took us on the grand tour of the facilities and she didn't miss one thing.

When it was time for lunch, we went into the dining room. Shelly pointed out her table. She had picked the flowers for the centerpiece and set the places. Her pride in her accomplishments, and that we were her guests, was touchingly obvious.

Later in her dorm I saw the Testament by her bed. On her dresser was the treasure box Dad made. Carefully she opened the lid and took out gifts for each of us. She had woven a place mat for Mom, and key chains for Dad, Jim, and myself. Now I understood that special look about her when we visited the arts and crafts shop; she had touched the loom as if it were an old friend.

As we thanked her for our gifts, Shelly stroked a lopsided pottery vase. Smiling and quiet, she seemed to be waiting for one of us to speak. It was Mom who finally got the picture, "You made that vase! Oh, Honey, you did it yourself! It's lovely, Shelly. We're so proud of you!"

Looking at Shelly, I thought, she's truly becoming a young woman. For the first time, she's relating to the world around her. She's even creating!

When it was time for us to leave, we gathered by the entrance to say good-bye. Although it was difficult leaving without Sis, it was not the heart-rending separation of a month before. And she would be coming home for a visit the following weekend.

After a round of hugs and kisses, we left Shelly and walked to the car. Suddenly Jimmy turned and ran back. Following a short distance behind, I could hear his voice clearly, "Sis, don't you miss living at home?" I stepped forward to intervene, afraid he might ruin the apparent adjustment Shelly had made. But before I could say anything, she replied matter of factly, "Nope."

Jimmy's face clouded. "But we love you!" he said almost pleadingly.

Shelly smiled and touched his head. "I love you, too.

I'll be home to visit." Then our doubts and fears were put to rest by Shelly's next words. Glancing contentedly about her, she declared, "I feel good here."

For several moments, Jimmy stood looking at his sister. Then he turned and started towards the car. As he passed by me, he smiled wistfully, "You were right, Junior. Sometimes the best decision is the hardest." Then he added a tender postscript, "for us . . . ."

18

STEWED TOMATOES

THE AROMA of fresh perked coffee enveloped me as I entered the new market. I was drawn to the coffee shop eager to relax and survey the hustle and excitement of others preparing for a busy day. Here I was with the entire morning to myself. Nothing, but nothing, was going to interfere with these hours of unhurried shopping.

As I slipped into a booth, sacks of money were being counted at the registers. Checkers prepared for early customers who were even now stalking the aisles for bargains.

Ummm, I thought, this coffee is as good as it smells.

I let my eyes wander about the bright new surroundings. A clerk hurried to finish a display of stewed tomatoes. Colorful signs with a catchy slogan proclaimed a new and better brand.

Guess I'll try some, I mused as I added "stewed tomatoes" to my shopping list.

Suddenly my tranquil scene was shaken by a loud, "What are those? What are you doing? Can I help? Here, I want to do it!" A young woman bombarded the clerk with questions and unsolicited help. There was something strangely different about her. Was she a comic reminder of a little child dressed in Mommy's clothes? But why should I have such an impression? She was meticuously dressed.

As the woman reached for another can, I noticed her

movements were oddly out of balance. She used only one arm while the other was cradled close to her body. Beginning to lose her balance, she straightened herself up, turned and started down the aisle.

She walked slowly, reaching for each step. The unevenness of her movements was obvious. Ah, that's it, I realized, her one leg is shorter than the other. Her careful step was for balance; she used her toes to equalize the difference in her legs.

Halfway down the aisle she turned back, pausing for a moment before continuing. That was when it finally registered. She's a child, I moaned, a child in an awkward adult body—oh, how sad!

Determined to shove the incident from my mind, I ordered two donuts and another cup of coffee. Wouldn't you know, I commiserated with myself, my first free morning in a month, and I have to run into this.

Finishing my snack, I set out to do my shopping. The tastefully arranged shelves soon had my full attention. My shopping cart was filling with the many things I needed, plus a few that I didn't. I was about to swing my basket up the next aisle, when I heard a voice call my name. Turning, I saw Ellen, an acquaintance. But wait—with her was that young woman. Then it dawned on me. The girl was Ellen's daughter!

My mind raced . . . look busy . . . read your list . . . stewed tomatoes, ground beef . . . don't look up . . . maybe she'll not pursue you . . . yuk . . . they're coming this way . . .

"Hello, Eunice. Do you like the new market?"

"Hi, Ellen," I replied. "I'm not sure. But they do have good donuts."

Slipping an arm around her daughter's waist, Ellen smiled at me, "Eunice, this is my daughter, Ann."

"Well," I stammered, "well, hello, Ann. I had no idea you were such a big girl." Why did I say that, I mentally kicked myself.

Ann stood looking at me. How could she be so controlled now, I wondered, when she was so childish just moments ago?

"We're shopping," Ann's voice interrupted my thoughts.

Laughing nervously, I fumbled for words, "Do you enjoy helping your mother?"

Ann stepped back from me. A piercing glance from her mother told her to remain quiet. She held her withered arm closer to her body and shifted her weight back and forth.

In the silence which followed I looked down at my feet, then at my cart, then at the shelves, then there were my feet again. I knew my face was the color of the can of stewed tomatoes atop my groceries.

Someone was prattling on and on too fast now. How irritating, I thought. It was me. I could hear myself saying, "Well, I must be off, so many things to do, nice to meet you, Pam."

"My name is *Ann*," was the sharp reply.

"I'm sorry, I'm just terrible with names," I called as I thrust my cart into action.

My beautiful morning destroyed, I stepped into a check-out line. As I moved slowly toward the register, I tried to interpret my feelings. Why did Ellen's daughter completely threw me? Why did I try to avoid meeting her? As the answers began to come, I blocked them from my mind. I didn't want to know. I just wanted to escape.

Squeaking cart wheels mingled with the din of cash registers. One sound rose above the noise of the busy store.

"Mama, that lady don't like me!"

Every muscle in my body tightened. "Don't turn," I warned. I didn't have to. Straight ahead in the large window was Ann's reflection, her good arm outstretched and pointing toward me . . . .

Hot tears blurred my hasty exit. Alone in my car, Ann's words burned in my mind. God, I cried, I didn't want to hurt her! And then I wondered, how often have other downcast eyes, turned-away faces, or retreating feet been just another painful rejection for a handicapped child?

So faith, hope, love abide, these
three; but the greatest of these is
love
(I *Corinthians* 13: 13 *RSV*).

THE INGREDIENT which makes faith and hope realities to the retarded is love. For God it is the most natural ingredient to provide. For man it is often the most difficult to receive and to share.

Before the retarded can comprehend the love of God, they must first experience the love of their fellowmen. They need to know that someone will touch them lovingly before they will believe that God would ever want to. And they need to know that someone will let them touch him also, for love to be love must be accepted as well as given.

Cheryl, herself physically and mentally handicapped, introduces a new friend, "This is Joan. She has trouble with her legs. I'm her helper." A child feeds another who cannot feed himself. A young man and woman walk hand-in-hand behind locked gates. The retarded comprehend love—they do experience it—for love not only covers a multitude of sins but a multitude of handicaps as well. We believe that as long as there is consciousness, love can be conveyed. And since God is love, He, too, then is conveyed through love which is dedicated to Him and given in His name.

It is only through the senses of the Lord that we can find and enjoy the loveliness of the person within when the outer wrapping is difficult to look upon.

If you would introduce the retarded to the Friend who will help shoulder their loneliness, frustration, and pain, and share their moments of happiness, you will need to draw upon every spiritual gift and resource within you. But remember—the first fruit of the spirit is love. If it is omitted the remaining fruits will lack flavor and fragrance—for love is the key to the door of the soul.

19

AMEN—AHEAD AND AT LAST!

I WAS SITTING in a folding chair, tense and uncomfortable, my mind trying desperately to disassociate itself from the present. Unrelated thoughts kept popping into my consciousness: write to Dad . . . forgot to defrost meat for dinner . . . wish the weather would warm up. My forced reverie was interrupted by loud piano music, accompanied by thirty-four enthusiastic voices. As if wanting to join in, weird howling began rising and falling from somewhere behind me, blowing an icy breath across my back. My natural impulse was to turn and look. Instead, I fastened my gaze on the soft, cool folds of the forest green stage curtain at the end of the room. My mind escaped again into a maze of thought. The events leading up to this moment flashed before me like stepping-stones falling into place across the past.

An amazing thing happened just a few short months before. I, Jane Dahl, became a Christian. It seemed incredible at my age—like falling in love for the first time at thirty-eight. On the heels of my excitement came a desire to serve the wonderful new Lord of my life. My decision to visit a special worship service for the mentally retarded was no casual choice. I had many hours of experience caring for my pretty little niece who was born with brain damage eight years before.

As the final stone fell into place bringing me up to the events of that day, I recalled arriving at church eager to meet the "children," as they were always referred to. Instead of the "little ones" I was expecting, a noisy, wild confusion burst through the doorway hand in hand with thirty-five assorted men and women, boys and girls. Although all were children mentally, most were adults. Many towered above my 5'1" frame.

What happened in the first moments that Wednesday afternoon seemed a frightening dream. I recoiled against the wall completely unprepared for this encounter and watched numbly as one young man, a mongoloid, stomped around the room on booted feet. He wore a toy holster and guns and blew gustily on a harmonica. A large woman, partially paralyzed, hugged everyone within reach. A horrible thought cut a painful path across my mind, "Would she come toward me with outstretched arms?" As if on cue, she turned and stared at me. Then, limping on mismatched legs, she came to gather me in her arms. A wet kiss shattered the vestiges of my composure.

One of the volunteers finally pried us apart. Relieved to see that the children were being encouraged to take their seats, I looked about for a place to collapse. It was then that I saw her.

She was olive skinned with owl-like features, and her straight black hair was cut in heavy bangs. Her body was twisted from the waist up in a diagonal swath from her left side to across her right shoulder. It was as if some unseen hand pushed upward against her back as she was being formed in her mother's womb. She darted furtively about, several magazines clutched beneath her arm. Now and then she would utter a chilling animal-like howl.

I gave her wide berth as I looked for a place to sit. I was still undone from my recent hugging match and was afraid I would lose control completely with any further contact. She scampered toward a table near the door, that unbelievable sound trailing behind her.

A movement down the aisle interrupted my thoughts as a volunteer left her chair to go to the rear of the room. I watched her bend down to the figure cringing beneath the table. She laid an arm gently across the deformed shoulders and spoke comfortingly. There was no response. "There never could be," I thought dismally.

My emotions riccocheted that day from revulsion to fear to pity to dismay. I wanted to run and never return. Instead, I sought comfort and strength from the Lord. And as I came back to Him again and again in prayer, I learned that being a Christian was not the easy bed of roses my early enthusiasm had pictured. There would be thorns along the way.

That first encounter with the children left my emotions pricked and bleeding, yet I felt compelled to return each week. If the service happened to be postponed, I was delighted. The love and pleasure the other women expressed in working with the children was beyond my comprehension. I was convinced I could never share their enthusiasm.

January, February, and March passed by, and April arrived in full bloom. We were at our usual posts one day preparing for "H" hour, the term I used privately to describe the children's arrival. Someone mentioned that one of the little girls, a spastic, was moving to another state.

"Oh, that's too bad," a voice rang out with sincerity, "it won't be as much fun without her!"

Startled, I looked to see who had spoken, but every eye turned toward me! The realization that my lips formed those memorable words hit me with tremendous impact. Something new and wonderful had blossomed, like spring, within my heart.

"I love these kids!" I shouted to myself.

All this time the Lord had been treating me for a coronary condition, and I hadn't realized until now that I was healed!

This experience proved to be a preview of another miraculous transformation that happened two years later when the Lord touched a second needy heart. The familiar Wednesday scene was unfolding. We were greeting the arriving children. Hugs and kisses were abounding, only now I was an instigator. Gradually I became aware of a friendly voice behind me mimicking my hellos. I turned, sensing something unusual was happening. My heart leaped as I saw the lone figure standing there, hunched and clutching her magazines as before. But she was different. For the first time her eyes mirrored an interest in the people and happenings about her. And she had spoken.

When the service began, she followed the other children to the rows of chairs at the front of the room, taking a seat across the narrow aisle from me. Not once did she look toward her favorite spot beneath the table. The awe which filled me minutes before was just beginning to subside, when God reached down to touch that moment again. We were praying the Lord's Prayer; the children's voices fumbled along the familiar closing line. Suddenly, the little crooked figure, perched expectantly on the edge of her chair, called out a loud "Amen!" a beat ahead of the rest of us.

The large room looked as it always had, with its rows of chairs creaking under the restless weight of children's bodies. But we were changed—she and I.

"Somewhere deep inside we are the same," I thought.

God, of course, had known this when He healed our hearts and filled them with His love.

> *A new heart I will give you, and a*
> *new spirit I will put within you;*
> *and I will take out of your flesh*
> *the heart of stone and give you*
> *a heart of flesh*
> *(Ezekiel 36: 26 RSV).*

20

RIGHT IN, RIGHT ON

THE BASKETBALL hit the rim, then bounced across the rough dirt surface of the playground. Terry hurried to retrieve it, his stocky adult body weaving back and forth behind the ball's erratic course.

I almost made a basket, he thought happily.

Only after the ball came to rest near the administration building, did he catch up with it. A few yards away he saw a small group of men huddled together in conversation. He recognized Timmy and Buck's fathers, but the third man he couldn't place. They were talking with Bob Carlson, the director of the school.

As Terry picked up the ball, he could hear their voices plainly, although he couldn't understand what they were talking about.

Timmy's father was speaking, "With tuitions going up the first of the year, we parents are anxious to cut expenses wherever possible. At our meeting last night, we decided to talk to you, Bob, about eliminating some of the children's activities, especially those that involve the bus."

"Yes," Buck's father interrupted, "gas, oil, insurance, and repairs have a way of adding up. To say nothing of the time involved for the driver and the house mothers and fathers who accompany the children."

"Well," Bob Carlson encouraged, "what do you suggest?"

"We want our kids to have every possible advantage," the third man spoke. "That is, experiences they can really profit from. But, frankly, Bob, we all question the value of their weekly visit to the church."

Terry had taken several steps towards the basketball court, but at the mention of "church," he stopped. They were speaking of something he understood after all. He continued to listen as Buck's father spoke again.

"We know our children better than anyone. We don't believe they get anything out of this religious program. They can't comprehend such deep concepts. And the crafts, games, punch, and cookies are not worth the time and expense involved in transporting them to and from the church each week."

Carlson raised a hand in emphasis. "I don't agree," he said. "The kids not only look forward to and enjoy this program, they also receive something very worthwhile. They do understand—in their own way—the Christian truths being taught. I believe they need this program."

Timmy's father shook his head. "I'm sorry, Bob, but you'll have to prove it to us. Otherwise, the program goes."

Terry sighed. It was all too much for him to follow. As he turned, bouncing the ball ahead of him, he heard Mr. Carlson say, "Why don't you ask one of the children what he thinks. Perhaps that will help you determine if the program has value or not."

Back on the smooth surface of the court, Terry held the ball at knee level, then with arms stiff as he swung it upwards and let it fly. The ball hit against the backboard, rolled along the rim, teetered back and forth, then plopped into the basket.

Looking around for witnesses to his victory, Terry saw the three fathers coming toward him. He hugged the ball to his chest and waited as they drew near.

"Well, Terry," Buck's dad said, "how are you?"

"Fine."

"Terry, we have a question or two we'd like to ask you. Okay?"

Oh, no, Terry thought. Why are people always asking me questions—what do you think about this? What do you think about that? He knew if he gave the answer they wanted, they would probably say, "Good boy, Terry!" or, "That's fine, Terry!" But if he didn't know the answer, they'd be disappointed. It was always the same.

"Terry," Buck's father continued, "did you go to church last week?"

Terry nodded.

Then more slowly and precisely, the father asked, "What did you learn in church last week?"

Terry set the ball down between his feet, straightened up, and replied, "God loves me!"

There was a long silence as the men stood looking at him. Terry wondered if he had given the right answer. Finally, Timmy's father smiled and patted him on the back. Then the three men turned toward the administration building where Bob Carlson was waiting.

As he picked up the ball again, Terry heard Buck's father. "Well, I'd say that was right to the heart of the matter. Let's tell Bob the program stays."

Terry lined himself up before the basket. He felt good. He was glad they hadn't asked him a hard question. Taking aim, he threw the ball toward the hoop. This time, right on target, it went in with a swoosh!

Make love your aim . . .
(I *Corinthians* 14: 1 *RSV*).

21

ONLY A PROMISE OF LOVE

THE COUPLE SAT on a bench in the school yard. Their arms were touching, their faces bright with the special joy of love. She was smiling, her head bent toward his conversation. "I wrote a song for you," he said.

Friends stopped to speak. A child interrupted noisily. But the two were locked in a private world.

The afternoon slipped away and as the shadows lengthened they talked of marriage—planned—dreamed —but their goal remained, as always, out of reach beyond tomorrow.

His mother came. With loving embrace she guided his sightless steps to the waiting car. The young woman walked beside him—both savoring the precious final moments together. Their hands touched—and he was gone.

There would never be more for them than this—a fleeting touch, a brief moment of companionship, a sharing of the need to be loved. For they are locked in still another world not of their choosing—a world which at birth rendered them physically and emotional-ly incapable of the greatest of human relationships.

She turned back to the bench alone. "I'll see him again tomorrow," she said softly.

God is love.

Man is created in His image.

God does not withhold His characteristic of love from any of His creation. For some with crippled minds and twisted bodies, love holds promise without fulfillment. Nevertheless it is love—answering a need for which it is given.

> "We love, because he first loved us (I John 4: 19 RSV).

22

THE RETRIEVED AND RELIEVED

THE SCENE was worthy of a Sherlock Holmes mystery. It was midnight, the sky an ebony arch overhead. The small bus stood like a yawning yellow bug, its front door slung open. Five cars crouched at the curb with headlights illuminating the unfolding drama. Figures scurried about, cutting through the shafts of light, then into the shadows—stopping to confer, then racing on in mounting frenzied activity. Fear was heavy on the air. One of the children was missing.

"Can you drive a load of kids to the rock concert Friday night?" Marge asked earlier that week. "Your main responsibility is to bring back the same number of children you take—not necessarily the same children, but the same number." This, she stressed, was the simplest way to avoid leaving anyone behind.

When the big night arrived, the kids were brushed, scrubbed, and dressed in their best, living testimonials to the loving care given by the busy house mothers and fathers. Eager for this special treat in their world of limited pleasures, they hurried into the waiting cars and school bus.

Happily their anticipation did not exceed the program. The rock group was the loud success the young in heart—and mind—enjoy. When the last amplified notes were rendered, wilted eardrums revived mid the shuffling sounds of feet moving toward the exits.

It was wild as the crowd spilled onto the lighted parking lot. Several minutes passed before each driver could verify that his number of children was present. By now it was after eleven. Sleepy kids slumped with heads resting against a window or a companion's shoulder as the caravan passed through dark and quiet neighborhoods.

Upon arriving at the school, each driver made one final check as the crumpled children tumbled out. It was at this point the driver of the bus made the frightening discovery—his count was short.

"But what could have happened?" someone shouted to no one in particular. "The count was right at the auditorium!"

An immediate recheck of the cars failed to uncover the missing child as an extra passenger elsewhere. By the process of elimination Marge determined it was Doreen who was lost—Doreen, a 32-year-old woman with the mentality of an 18-month-old baby.

For years Doreen came to the weekly worship service only to withdraw behind a barrier of indifference. Every effort of love to break through to the "person within" failed. Then just recently a noticeable change occurred. Doreen began to respond. Now she was somewhere in the night, alone.

Although the driver was certain Doreen entered the bus following the performance, Marge and three others returned to the auditorium. The parking lot was now dark and deserted, the surrounding walnut trees ominous and foreboding. What if Doreen had wandered into the orchard? What if someone saw her—followed her? Each searcher was haunted by a mental picture of some potential horror.

Marge pleaded silently, Dear God . . .

Suddenly a voice whispered, "Wha . . . what's that?"

"It sounds like music!" Marge answered, her eyes wide and staring.

Huddling close, they picked their way to the auditorium which was dark except for a slit of light beneath the entrance. Waiting, they listened.

"It is music!" a housefather croaked.

Pulling open the double doors, they came upon the rock group giving a command performance for one lone music lover. In the front row, swaying in time with the music, sat Doreen.

It didn't take much doing to piece together what had happened. Doreen entered the bus all right. Somehow she sensed it wouldn't leave without her. But once on board and counted, she walked to the back and out the rear exit! Returning undetected to the auditorium, she found a choice seat front and center.

When the musicians came on stage to retrieve their equipment, there was a small but determined audience waiting. Unable to discover who she was or where she belonged, they decided to act as musical babysitters until someone came to claim her. They even presented her with their autographed record album.

It seemed incredible the young men could feel such compassion for Doreen. Not that her physical and mental handicaps would turn them away, but her lack of warmth would. Marge was pondering this when one of the musicians made a revealing remark, "We dug her friendliness."

A few weeks earlier, Doreen began to peck her way out of her silent shell. Now she was making further progress. She was giving of herself—not just in response to the giving of others—she had taken the initiative and reached out in friendship. Yes, the weeks, months, and years of persistent love were finally bearing fruit.

Back at the school and tucked in bed, Doreen slept like a baby, the album clutched beneath her arm. But for those who searched that night with fearful hearts, sleep did not come until dawn had bleached the dark horizon gold.

Love is patient; love is kind and envies no one. Love is never boastful, nor conceited, nor rude; never selfish, not quick to take offence. Love keeps no score of wrongs; does not gloat over other men's sins, but delights in the truth. There is nothing love cannot face; there is no limit to its faith, its hope, and its endurance (I Corinthians 13: 4-7 NEB).

23

THAT'S WHERE IT'S AT

THE LIGHTS of the school are bright against the dark night. Parents and friends arrive in the small parking lot at the front of the new facility. Several children wait near a tall chain-link gate to usher guests down the walkway, past the dining hall, and into the multipurpose room.

"Hi, we're having a show!" a handsome youth exclaims, shaking every willing hand.

Inside the large rectangular room, twenty rows of chairs face a curtain. A feeling of expectation wanders noisily up and down the aisles. The houselights dim. A hush falls. The curtain opens and the play begins.

The scene is a small gift shop. The children are dressed in pink, red, and white, their faces the centers of beautiful lace and paper valentines. Like a row of greeting cards placed along a shelf, they are seated on a bench across the rear of the stage.

A narrator reads from a script as a young man enters, "Johnny has come to buy a valentine for his sweetheart."

Johnny considers each card carefully, makes his selection, and leaves. Other shoppers come and go until all of the valentines are gone—all except one. It is not pretty like the others. It is "The Ugly Valentine."

"The little lone card is crying because it has not been chosen," the narrator says sadly.

There is a tender truth to the story. All of the performers are mentally retarded—many physically handicapped as well.

Suddenly music brightens the scene, and children dressed in red leotards dance to "Love, Sweet Love." The song ends and the mood changes as couples move slowly to a romantic waltz. Each number emphasizes the happy theme "Sweethearts in Love." It is touchingly apparent that for many this type of love will forever remain a mystery; and for those who can understand, it will never become a reality.

The director steps forward.

"The kids chose this next song themselves," he explains, "it has a special meaning."

Onto the stage troops the entire cast. Holding hands or with arms entwined they proclaim, "Jesus loves the little children . . . all the children of the world . . . red and yellow, black and white, they are precious in His sight . . . Jesus loves the little children of the world."

For the first time the program has real meaning for the performers. Here is love they can understand—a love that imposes no impossible burdens, no discriminating restrictions, no eliminating conditions. Here is a perfect, divine love, offered simply, its only contingency an accepting heart.

The moment ends. The stage is empty. To the center walks a young woman. Her high untrained voice rings plaintively as she ponders, "Where is love?"

The kids have already answered that timeless question. "Jesus loves . . ." their song began. Jesus loves—*that's* where it's at!

> *Herein is love, not that we loved*
> *God, but that he loved us*
> (I *John* 4: 10).

24

HELP TODD NOW

BLOOD SEEPING from the wound had coagulated about the sutures that seemed to hold the child's head together. Only an intense blow with a dull object could possibly have caused such a wound. Bill seemed proud of the artwork that stood out so boldly on his shaved head. While the housefather, John, was giving his version of the accident, Bill who could neither hear nor speak wasn't having any trouble communicating. These two had burst through the door almost running me down as I waited for any latecomers. There was Bill, eager to display himself, with John half a step behind to assure me that, though wounded, Bill was doing very well and wouldn't miss this opportunity for the world. Before I had adjusted to the shock or even given my stomach a chance to return to its normal residing place, Bill lurched forward pointing an accusing finger at Todd. Every eye was riveted on Bill's gestures as he showed us how he had been bashed, laid low, rescued and stitched together. And to my shame, I sent a disapproving glare in Todd's direction, whose agony could be felt from across the room. John hastened to tell me of Bill's gross misbehavior. For weeks he'd been asking for trouble. I could vouch for that fact. He had been unruly and disruptive at worship for several weeks—pinching, pushing, intruding into private conversations with loud guttural sounds, then asking forgiveness with bear hugs and wet kisses.

Bill was a beautiful child who in spite of his unpredictable behavior was loved and accepted by everyone. But anyone disrupting the weekly worship met with disapproval. All other activities for these children revolved around this service. It was such a happy day for them and us too as we shared their enthusiasm.

The call to worship sounded. Bill chose to sit near the door. That door just happened to be as far from Todd as was possible. There would be about twenty minutes for me to gather my thoughts together before the lesson time. Seated apart from the group, I began to reconstruct the day. All morning I had been restless and irritable which was the outgrowth of trying to involve and interest those few students who just sat. Arriving at church a bit late I found half a dozen helpers busy preparing for the worship service. Expectantly we gathered near the door awaiting the children's arrival, poised as if a large wave were about to break over us. And then it did! Children descended upon us with the abandon of a litter of pups—each one striving for a place . . . eager to be greeted . . . to be looked at . . . to be touched . . . even hugged or kissed. Many so inarticulate that their best means of communication was body contact; with a few of the large adults it was almost body combat. How else can you express such childlike exuberance when you are held captive in a damaged container? Each one different, yet trying desperately to convey the same message, "Look at me! Here I am! Please don't turn away or draw back."

Todd had arrived late, head down, pushing his way through the group still gathered at the door. Strange behavior for Todd who was almost always first to arrive with an outstretched hand and a shy smile that brightened his mongoloid features. He would eagerly share some special event in his life since last we met. And then there it would be the frustration of my own inadequacy. "What's the use? Should he be down the hall in the playroom?" I could see Todd from where I was seated. He was as unresponding as the chair he always sat in. Just a constant rock to and fro. How long had he been rocking while the others were coming to know Christ? One year—two? "What do I think I'm doing!" Discouragement seemed to envelop me. My heart cried out to the Lord, "If only Todd had understood some of these last few lessons, today might have been different. What will he do with the guilt and the agony he is suffering?"

For weeks our lessons had dealt with burdens, you name it and there it was gathered together in one room. Just pick a burden—fear, rejection, a crippled mind or body, or the weight of a wrong decision. Oh, we had established what a burden was, and discovered they did not discriminate as to size, color, or capabilities. This series had started by acting out a scene. The setting was the grocery store, completely stocked with all manner of packaged and canned goods. A helper was needed to carry my groceries. There was an eager volunteer who smilingly offered to help. As the bag got heavier the expression and eagerness of my friend soon changed to one of disbelief. However, he was determined to keep his word no matter what the cost and he had made a grand effort. No one could possibly have carried that load for long. The floor shook as the bag came down with a thud! His face told the story—such relief, how good to be rid of it, to rest and be aware of other things; and there are so many other things to be aware of, beautiful things that we miss when our burden is too heavy.

As I walked forward for the lesson there were friendly smiles, whispered hellos, and occasionally an outstretched hand to be touched or squeezed. How could I be discouraged with all this love surrounding me?

"Oh, Father, we claim your promise that where two or three are gathered together, there you will be also." Traveling through the familiar lesson I soon found myself summing up, challenging. "Did you come today with a burden? Have you made a wrong choice? Is this the day you will call out and say, 'Here I am, Lord'? Remember the little lost lamb? When he called out, the shepherd found him and lifted him tenderly in his arms. Trust the Lord to treat you tenderly. He is always forgiving, always loving." Our eyes met—Todd's and mine. There was that look of agony still. I had an almost irresistible urge to gather him into my arms and brush the moist dark curls from his forehead. "Help him, Lord! Help Todd now." The room was silent except for the loud pounding of my heart. Then it happened. Todd's movement slowed and then stopped. He rose to his feet and came forward. Standing firmly planted in front of everyone, head bowed, hands clasped, his voice was strong and clear, "Forgive me, Lord. I've hurt my friend. I'm sorry, please make him better." My body was trembling as tears of joy spilled unashamedly down my cheeks. My arm slipped about his shoulders as he looked into my face. Todd was radiant. There was a twinkle in his dark eyes and a beautiful big grin on that sweet face. Looking up, Todd could see Bill's face reflecting his new peace and joy. Forgiveness was truly complete—human and divine. Praise the Lord!

> *Come to me, all who labor and are heavy-laden, and I will give you rest. Take my yoke upon you, and learn from me; for I am gentle and lowly in heart, and you will find rest for your souls. For my yoke is easy, and my burden is light*
>
> (*Matthew* 11: 28-30 *RSV*).

25

SHALOM—BUT HANUKKAH!

"JESUS—THAT NAME isn't allowed to be spoken in our house!" the words flew like darts from Mrs. Goldstein's mouth. "We simply will not permit Dannie to take part in a program about Jesus. Just because our son is at your school doesn't mean you have the license to indoctrinate him in a belief contrary to his family's. Our sacred holiday is Hanukkah—not Christmas!"

I was stunned by this outburst. Normally my confrontations were with children. Not with mothers.

Forcing a smile, I apologized, "I'm sorry if we offended you. We encouraged Dannie to take part in our Christmas pageant not realizing he was Jewish." In the silence that followed, my smile began to wilt around the edges.

Waiting for her to reply, I wondered how the fact of Dannie's Jewish background escaped us. He had come to our class three months ago. At that time we were taking our weekly worship service to the children at their residence school. Dannie had wandered into the multipurpose room during our craft time one afternoon. I noticed him immediately. He was tall, heavy set, and in his early twenties. A quiet, well-mannered boy, his physical disabilities seemed greater than his mental handicap. As I thought back, I recalled asking him his name. All he had given me was "Dannie." Somehow I failed to inquire later about his family or surname. When there are thirty to thirty-five retarded students to minister to, you sometimes neglect the amenities.

That first day, Dannie's personality and sense of humor were enhancing additions, and we happily received him into our class. Two weeks later as we picked the children for the nativity scene he seemed a natural for one of the three wisemen. Oi vey!

Now I searched for some way to explain to his mother that the love expressed through Christmas poses no threat, but instead holds the promise of peace on earth and goodwill for *all* men.

Finally I broke the silence, "I do respect the Jewish faith, Mrs. Goldstein. Remember, we worship the same God."

"The same God, yes," she replied, the iciness thawing from her manner, "but not Jesus."

As we discussed the pageant further, its importance to the children, not only as an expression of faith, but as a means of sharing the joy and love that uniquely permeate this holiday, we found ourselves on common ground in the God of the Old (and New!) Testament. When we parted that afternoon, Mrs. Goldstein said she would discuss Dannie's possible participation with her husband.

The night of the pageant at last arrived. My annual case of the butterflies was not as pronounced as usual. God had already worked one miracle and I was confident He could manage two or three more—the minimum number essential for a successful program!

As I approached the church hall that evening, there was Dannie, handsome in a charcoal suit, white shirt, and red bow tie, seated at a small table just inside the entrance. His loving nature had already attracted several young people from among the early arrivals.

When he saw me, Danny straightened importantly in his chair. Carefully he selected a program from the neat pile on the table before him. Holding it out, he turned it rightside up toward me. I reached to take it, looking down at the tiny creche on the cover with the single shining star above.

As I passed into the hall I heard him call after me, "Shalom and Happy Hannukah, Dorothy!"

Turning, I called back, "Shalom and Merry Christmas, Dannie!"

The Lord our God is one Lord
(Deuteronomy 6: 4).

26

CLOTHES MAKE THE WOMAN

MY REFLECTION in the mirror was perfect. I've done it at last, I complimented myself, no one will recognize me in this outfit!

Covered from head to toe with large paper bags, there was not one bit of me showing. This, plus the fact I was more devious than previous Halloweens, would make my disguise an impenetrable mystery.

I drove to church with my costume beside me. Finding an empty room, I dressed carefully, lining up the two openings with my eyes so I could see. I waddled down the corridor to the office. Once inside, I paused at the counter and waited for Lil to look up from her typewriter.

"What!" she exclaimed, then broke into prolonged guffaws.

I remained silent.

"Who are you?" she stopped laughing long enough to ask.

I merely shrugged.

Looking me over thoroughly, she tried to guess my identity, "You're Ernie! (the janitor) . . . Ned (a minister) . . . Not Carol (another secretary)!"

Finally I spoke, "Happy Halloween, Lil!" My voice was muffled through the thick paper.

It was several moments before she shouted, "Dorothy —it's you!"

"Well," I asked, "do you think the kids will know who I am this time?"

"Absolutely not!" was her encouraging reply.

I needed that encouragement. Each year I dressed in an elaborate disguise to fool the kids at the Halloween party. Each year one of the children—usually John—quickly penetrated my masquerade. But this year would be different. I was completely camouflaged!

With Lil's reassuring words to motivate me, I toddled confidently up the corridor to the Fellowship Hall, then into the adjacent kitchen to hide. After children arrived and activities began, I planned to slip into the hall and stand quietly, but prominently, amongst them. Since seven or eight other women as well as the kids, would be in costume, I was sure no one would know who I was.

Suddenly I heard voices, laughter, and music coming through the closed door between the hall and kitchen. The children had arrived. Waiting several minutes, I stepped through the door. Moving along the wall, I ventured toward the center of the room and stopped. Kids were involved in bean bag toss, bobbing for apples, fishing for prizes, and having makeup applied by two volunteers. As I stood there perfectly still, Mollie wandered up, peered intently into my eye slits, then turned and left.

Aha, I thought, she didn't know me!

One of the little children brushed by, stopped, and poked a finger into the sack covering my legs and feet. Apparently satisfied I was a dummy, he ran off to take a turn at the apples.

Out of the corner of my eye I saw John ambling toward me. Oh, oh, I thought, here comes the acid test. This young man had penetrated every one of my previous disguises. But I was confident I had him this time. And how I would enjoy his surprised expression when I unveiled later!

"Well, well," John said in happy recognition, "how are you, Dorothy?"

Then before I could recover and reply he added,

"You've never looked better!" As he spoke, he punctuated his remarks with a slap on my back that bent me double.

Slowly I lifted the crumpled bag from over my head and shoulders. "How in the world did you know it was me?" I grumbled.

"Why, Dorothy," he chortled, wagging a finger in my face, "I'd know you anywhere!"

27

HOW DO YOU KNOW I LOVE YOU?

HER HANDS PUSHED and pressed against the earth. As she worked, Dorothy looked about the garden. Along one side of the house, camellias and azaleas alternated places in a long procession of color. From a shady corner, pink and lavender rhododendrons announced an early spring. To her left stood the dogwood tree, nodding in lacy majesty to the wind. Its cross-shaped blossoms were stark white against the dark and aged trunk of an oak.

How can anyone with eyes not believe in God, she pondered.

"Oh!" she said aloud, as inspiration for a lesson came. Rushing into the house for pen and paper, she shook her head in wonder at God's constant provision of ideas.

Returning with the writing supplies, she jotted down the first thought, "If you have eyes, you can *see* God's love."

We'll take the children for a nature walk around the church grounds, she decided, and relate the beauty of the flowers to God's love. It was out of love, after all, that He created the world for them to enjoy.

The next idea came quickly. She scribbled it beneath the first, "If you have hands, you can *touch* God's love." Perhaps, she thought, I can involve the women in this one. They can mingle with the children expressing love through hugs and pats. What an enthusiastic response this will bring, she imagined.

The third and fourth points came in rapid succession: if you have ears, you can *hear* God's love; if you have a heart, you can *feel* God's love. The third point was not difficult to illustrate. She had albums of beautiful music for the children to listen to. Reading I Corinthians 13 would be good, too. "And I'll bring the neighbor's singing canary!" she said, snapping her fingers at the idea.

It was the fourth point that gave her difficulty. How could she illustrate that God's love is felt through the heart? The children knew what love was. They experienced it. But the objects of their affection had substance —substance they could see, touch, or hear. God didn't exactly fit 'into any of those categories. Somehow she must help them understand that they have "inside" and "outside" feelings; that with outside feeling they discover evidence of God's love, and with inside feeling they experience God's love for themselves.

She decided to take cold, hot, hard, and soft items for the children to touch. This would help them to understand outside feeling. But as she arrived at church the following week, she was still not sure she could adequately explain inside feeling. This lesson may require three or more class sessions to cover, she thought, as she drew pictures of a hand, an ear, an eye, and heart on the blackboard.

When it was time to begin, she pointed to her artwork explaining, "God made us and the world around us so that we can see, touch, hear, and feel His love." Using the records, the Bible, the canary—who fortunately co-operated—the pictures, and the women's sensitivity session, she proceeded to illustrate her statement.

Then as she began what she hoped was her clinching-the-lesson conclusion, she directed the children to blow against their hands.

"Can you *feel* your breath?" she asked.

Heads nodded in reply.

"Can you *see* your breath?"

Now there were nods, puzzled expressions, and head-shaking indicating that it was impossible.

"We can't *see* God, but we can *feel* His love—just as we can't see our breath against our hand, but can feel it." She looked about the class for signs of understanding.

There was David, a young man with the intelligence of half his twenty years, nodding and smiling. Dorothy felt hope blossoming. Walking over to David she asked, "How do you know I love you, David?"

At once the other children twisted in their chairs to watch and listen. To them, David was a celebrity. He could play the piano by ear. All they had to do was "hum a few bars" and off he would go. His retardation made the accomplishment extraordinary. The fact he was born blind made it remarkable.

"Well, Dorothy, I know. Yes, I know," he said in his peculiar, decisive, repetitive way. "I know just because I know. I know."

"Yes," Dorothy encouraged, "but *how* do you know? You can't see me." He doesn't understand, after all, she sighed.

Then with all eyes turned in his direction, David placed his hand on his chest. "I know you love me, Dorothy, I know. I know because I feel your love—here!"

What a powerful illustration, thought Dorothy, as she felt again the thrill of breakthrough. She realized, however, that David's understanding was the culmination, not of this one lesson, but of many acts of love. She recalled a handicapped friend guiding David down the ramp from the dorms, a protective arm about his waist; a housefather teaching him to be self-reliant, not as part of his job, but because he cared; and the ladies bringing countless cupcakes and cookies to add a bit of brightness to his dark world.

How constant is God's love pouring through us, thought Dorothy. And each time we convey His love to these children, we convey Him, also. Because God *is* love!

Beloved, let us love one another;
for love is of God, and he who
loves is born of God and knows
God. He who does not love does
not know God; for God is love
            (I *John* 4: 7, 8 *RSV*).

28

A RELUCTANT VOLUNTEER

THAT MORNING Bob's wife, with obviously planned casualness, dropped the bomb. She had voluntereed him to help with the Christmas program.

"You've got to be kidding," he gasped, his head snapping with each word. Bob never could understand why she worked with the retarded. He was even less equipped to visualize himself doing so. The thought of being hugged and touched by those affectionate children actually frightened him.

"No, Honey," he said with finality, "no way!"

But after a week of his favorite foods, no complaints at his watching football all weekend, and a smiling, loving response to his every mood, Bob knew the battle was lost. He decided not to acknowledge defeat. Maybe she'll forgot the whole thing, he reasoned hopefully.

But the following Monday, intuitively aware of her victory, she began outlining his duties. First, he would not have to attend rehearsals. "Great!" Second, he would operate the spotlight from the audience. "Check." Third, simple typed instructions would be given him. "Fine." And fourth, he would not have to attend the children's party afterwards. "Perfect!"

The next two weeks passed with amazing speed. And then it was the night of the program. They drove separately to church since Bob would be returning home before his wife. In the hallway she breezed by him on a last minute errand, pausing long enough to peck him on the cheek and hand him his instructions. Looking them over he found they were quite simple. Well, he thought, it figures—simple people, simple program, simple instructions.

Tucking the paper into his shirt pocket, he noticed a small attractive woman welcoming people at the entrance. She looked normal enough to Bob, but then you couldn't always tell. He returned her "hello," carefully avoiding her outreached hand.

"Good evening, Mrs. Stoddard," a voice behind him greeted the woman. Oh, oh, Bob moaned silently, the minister's wife! Well, it was old-fashioned to shake hands anyway.

Inside the hall a goodly crowd was finding seats. Bob slipped down a narrow side aisle to where the spotlight perched precariously atop a table. Easing himself up alongside it, he found his pedestal surprisingly steady. Thank goodness for that much, he sighed to himself. Studying his instructions, he moved the light around making certain he understood each direction.

As he experimented with the equipment, he saw his wife hurrying towards the door leading to backstage. Catching her eye, he formed a circle with his thumb and first finger. Nodding back, she pushed against the door and was gone; just then the houselights dimmed and darkness closed about him.

Searching in the dark, Bob found a flashlight in a box near his feet. He fondled its cool, smooth surface—a pacifier in his unsteady hands—while he watched the curtain slowly opening to reveal a lighted stage.

In the scene before him, a grandmother sat in a rocking chair, a Bible open on her lap. Behind her a man was decorating a tree. Sitting at the grandmother's feet was a small child. At a table two women strung white puffs of popcorn on long strings. Bob's wife had told him one of the women in the scene was a volunteer. The rest of the players were retarded. He couldn't remember which was which, and for the life of him he couldn't tell by

114

looking. Well, it isn't important, he consoled himself.

"It is Christmas Eve," a narrator began speaking into a microphone offstage. "While the family is preparing for Christmas morning, grandmother reads aloud from her Bible, 'I bring you good tidings of great joy, which shall be to all people. For unto you is born this day in the city of David a Saviour, which is Christ the Lord. And this shall be a sign unto you; Ye shall find the babe wrapped in swaddling clothes, lying in a manger.'"

When the curtain was closed again, Bob heard scenery and props being pushed to one side. Recalling what his wife said earlier, that would be the kids from the high school department. In an age that placed such importance on appearance, personality, and intelligence, Bob found the high schoolers' involvement with the retarded hard to compute.

When it was finally quiet backstage, the recorded voice of Bing Crosby began crooning the virtues of a white Christmas. Immediately Bob responded to his first cue: Swing spotlight toward back of hall; switched it on. There coming through the two main entrances were small groups of men, women, boys, and girls. These were the ones too mentally or physically handicapped to participate on stage. Some were pulled in wagons, others were led by volunteers. Each wore a knitted scarf and cap. Running in and around the would-be carolers was a little six-year-old dressed as a snowflake. When prompted, she tossed a handful of artificial snow into the air.

The snow ran out about the same time as Bing. Children and volunteers then went around the large room encouraging the audience to join in caroling. As they ended a lively rendition of "Jingle Bells," the little groups left, waving and calling "Merry Christmas!" It was difficult keeping the spotlight on the moving figures, but all in all Bob was satisfied with his effort.

The next several scenes were not so demanding. Bob sneaked a look at his watch, shielding the flashlight's beam from the audience with his body. The program had been in progress thirty-five minutes. He checked his instructions. Only one scene left to go. Slipping a piece of blue cellophane over the face of the spotlight, he waited with thumb on switch.

As the final curtain opened, Bob flipped on the light. He felt a tinge of pride as the stage shimmered in a soft, moonlight effect. A young woman was seated on a low stool, a shawl draped around her head and shoulders. In her arms, wrapped in the unlikely folds of a pastel striped receiving blanket, she cuddled the stiff form of a doll. Her radiant face was bent toward the "baby." Kings and shepherds knelt at her feet. One king, a big, curly-headed boy, rocked back and forth, back and forth, back and forth. The other children remained completely still. Very effective, Bob admitted silently.

A choir of eight men and women were singing "O Holy Night" from risers to the left of the stage. When the last notes faintly lingered on the air, Bob switched off the spotlight, relieved his responsibilities were over. He found, however, the program was not. House and stage lights now illuminated the hall. A Christmas tree at the front of the room was lit. Coming through the entrances were the children from the earlier caroling scene.

There were the wagons carrying their pathetic cargoes —the volunteers tugging and pushing those able to walk. Each child carried a gift. Some brought gaily wrapped packages, others a single flower. At the stage they placed their gifts at the feet of the mother and child. And all the while they were singing "Happy birthday to You, happy birthday to You, happy birthday, dear Jesus, happy birthday to You."

Bob felt something sliding down his face. He hunched his shoulder, turned his head and pressed his cheek against his jacket, keeping his hands stuffed nonchalantly in his pockets. He had to repeat the procedure several times before the last child had offered his gift and left. Then Pastor Stoddard gave the benediction. Well, thought Bob, it was a tear-jerking finale all right. Climbing from the table, he made his way to the corridor. The exit to the parking lot was jammed with people. As he stood unable to move forward, he noticed an open door across the hall. He slipped through hoping to find a quiet place to wait until the crowd thinned out.

The room he entered was cluttered, brightly lit, and appeared to be empty. Racks of clothes stood along one wall. "This is where the kids were dressed for the program," he muttered to himself. "After their party they'll be back for their final change."

Walking to the center of the room, Bob stood gazing down at the rug. His thoughts and feelings were in perpetual motion. He tried to calmly evaluate his emotions, but the children kept coming into his mind. He saw them bringing their gifts to the Christ Child, a joy and light in their faces that could not be denied. Sure, there were some unresponsive ones. But most of them seemed to understand what they were doing—and why!

Suddenly he felt an arm slip around his waist. He turned expecting to see his wife. But, no, he remembered seeing the face that stared up at him in the caroling scene. A volunteer had pulled her up the aisle, her twisted body struggling to keep up.

Bob backed away but the arm hung on, tightening its grip. Daring another look into that face, he saw a pair of sparkling brown eyes and a wide mouth stretched into a grin. Although there were strings of drool like a teething baby, the grin was ingratiating. Bob found himself grinning back! At that instant, his fear succumbed to compassion. And there was no one more surprised than Bob!

When his wife, following the sound of his laughter, entered the room, Bob and his friend were romping like frisky fawns. Unable at first to comprehend what she was seeing, she gradually realized her husband was playing tag with one of the children. She watched spellbound as Bob patted the girl on the head then moved around outside her reach while she lumbered happily after him. He swung around, saw his wife, and stopped short just as the lumbering figure lunged at him. The two playmates collided. Grasping one another around

117

the neck, they clung together to keep from falling. And then the three of them were laughing, laughing, laughing . . . .

Later at home, Bob tried to express his feelings to his wife, but the love being born within him was too embryonic yet to be spanked into verbal expression. So, instead, he turned the conversation toward her.

"I know now why you work with the retarded," he said almost shyly.

"You do?"

"It's because they're people like us, with needs the same as ours."

"Yes."

There was a period of silence.

"Honey," he said softly, "I had a very nice time tonight."

> *Little children, let us not love in word or speech but in deed and in truth.*
>
> (I *John* 3: 18 *RSV*).

Look at me
  Look at me
    Don't turn away!

Touch me, please
  Touch me, please
    Kneel with me, pray.

Your needs
  Are my needs
    For
      Faith
        Hope
          and
            Love.

Your source
  Is my source—
    Our Father above.

Share with me
  Share with me
    What you believe.

I, too, in
  Humbleness
    Christ can receive.

29

A LOOK AT DISCIPLINE

As THE PARENT or teacher of a retarded child, have you ever found yourself on the receiving end of the lesson rather than on the giving end? One of the times this happened to me involved, of all things, a point of discipline.

It all began during the craft time one afternoon. I was passing out materials when Joe, one of the teenage boys, decided to try out for the Bolshoi Ballet. Had it been one of the smaller boys, I would have picked him up and set him in a chair. Joe's six-foot frame prevented that, however.

So, instead, I rushed across the room and planted myself in the path of the stomping, yelling youth. "If you don't stop this racket at once," I warned, "I'm going to wup you!"

My words had an unexpected effect. Like a balloon expelling air in frantic flight, Joe whirled to a gradual stop. "What," he asked, "is 'wup'?"

His puzzled expression caught me off guard. In the momentary calm that followed, Joe grabbed my arm. "Now, now, Dorothy," he cooed soothingly, "take it easy. Everything is going to be all right."

I had used those same words time and again to comfort an unhappy, frustrated child. Now Joe was using them to comfort me instead!

Later, with the incident fresh in my mind, I decided to take another look at discipline. As with previous perusals, I began with the "whys" of disciplining. Here are some of the ideas I jotted down:

A positive approach to discipline can make a dramatic difference in a parent or teacher's ability to relate to a retarded child. As with normal children, the mentally handicapped are more content, and better adjusted when reasonable boundaries have been established. These boundaries provide needed security, and as a result the disciplined child is more trusting of and responsive to those involved with his care and instruction. When discipline has been established and is a familiar part of the child's training, the resultant benefits will not be limited to the child alone. The parent or teacher's attitude will brighten when he knows he has control due to the child's prior disciplinary training.

Next I went to the dictionary to see what it gave as the definition of discipline. There were three main points: 1. Training of the mental, moral, and physical powers by instruction, control, and exercise; 2. The state or condition of orderly conduct, etc., resulting from such training; and, 3. Punishment or disciplinary action for the sake of training or correction. From its definition, then, discipline is not a negative concept, but involves conscientious attention which the retarded need and deserve.

Turning from the dictionary to the Bible, I found God had much to say about discipline.

> *Train up a child in the way he*
> *should go: and when he is old, he*
> *will not depart from it*
> > (*Proverbs* 22: 6).

Whoso loveth instruction loveth knowledge: but he that hateth reproof is brutish

(*Proverbs* 12: 1).

Withhold not correction from the child . . .

(*Proverbs* 23: 13).

Exercise thyself rather unto godliness

(I *Timothy* 4: 7).

These verses clearly state that discipline is beneficial, necessary, and commanded of God. God, the ultimate authority, passes His authority to us for the purpose of training those for whom we are responsible. So, the key to successful disciplining is in appropriating God's authority, through prayer: "Lord, this child is beyond my control. Give me Your wisdom, love, and authority (power) to help him learn to behave well."

I also found that in Hebrews (12: 10, 11) it speaks of God's discipline as an act of love toward His children so that they may share His holiness. We should keep this worthy aim in mind when God uses us as His instruments in disciplining.

From what I have read in the dictionary and the Bible, I have developed a few simple rules. These methods are not necessarily successful with every child. As with the normal, each one is different and requires individual consideration.

1. *Be loving.* Before a child will respect your authority, he must know that you love him and have his best interests at heart. To maintain a loving attitude, have control over the child's behavior. Children soon recognize that discipline, applied prayerfully and carefully, is a form of love.

The day I had my confrontation with Joe, I was not applying this first rule. Joe sensed in my anger a lack of love. Not until that anger subsided were Joe and I able to communicate.

In similar situations, when you feel pushed to your emotional limits, it helps to remember that Christ accepts us as we are. He has forgiven us of our sins—past, present, and future. He disciplines us with patience and love. We can, through prayer and dedication, apply His acceptance, patience, and love to those He entrusts to our care.

2. *Be kind.* Always give the child ample opportunity to correct his behavior himself. Where deep emotional problems exist, additional time and effort may be necessary. For example, if the child is hyperactive, a walk out of doors, and a quiet talk about God's love, your love, and the importance of being considerate, can help the child to settle down.

It is often helpful to put your arm about the child's shoulders or (as Joe did with me!) take the child's arm in a firm but loving gesture. The retarded generally desire to be touched. This helps them to understand that it is not they you are finding unacceptable, but their behavior.

3. *Be fair.* When dealing with an adult with the mentality of a five-year-old, discipline him at his mental age level, not his numerical age level.

Never set unreasonable boundaries that will frustrate and discourage the child. But rather be encouraging—not only when his behavior improves, but also when he tries yet fails.

Bobby, numerically twelve but mentally two, was giving me a difficult time one day. I spent the better part of the hour running down the hall after him. I would bring him back to class, only to have him run off again the minute my back was turned. Finally, he hid himself in the nursery behind the cribs. Just as I discovered his hiding place, the janitor appeared on the scene. He had heard me calling Bobby. "Do you want me to deal with the young man?" he volunteered. But Bobby was my responsibility. I knew that for his sake, as well as my own, I must find a solution. So, I marched him down the hall as before, but this time I didn't scold or try to explain why his behavior was unacceptable. When we got back to the classroom, I sat him in a chair next to me. Every time he made a move to rise, I put my hands on his shoulders and pushed him down again. Finally, he was quiet. I watched him closely. When he began getting restless, I told him he could get up as long as he remained in the room. From then on, whenever the wanderlust hit him, I merely had to point to a chair. With me, at least, Bobby's wandering problem was over.

4. *Be consistent.* Once reasonable boundaries have been established, be firm in your resolve that the child remain within them. All children test authority to see if it can be penetrated. If you allow the child to succeed, you encourage him to ignore the boundaries. As a result, your authority becomes ineffectual. Of course unusual circumstances occasionally arise when boundaries need to be temporarily relaxed. A child may have been given a new medication which affects his behavior beyond his control. Or he may be upset because a friend has rejected him. Such instances provide opportunities for the parent or teacher to pray with the child about the difficulty.

Realizing it is not always easy to recall a long list of rules when faced with an immediate behavior problem, I also worked out some A, B, C's that may be of help until you are better established in a pattern of disciplining.

A. Ask the child in a loving but firm manner to correct his behavior.

B. Be certain he understands his actions are not acceptable (disturbing to the class, harmful to himself).

C. Clearly explain what the consequences will be if he fails to obey (he will be taken from the room, he cannot participate in the refreshment time, he cannot watch television, you will speak to his parents, he will not be allowed to return to class, or whatever you feel is right for that child).

D. Do carry out whatever disciplinary action is necessary for the sake of his training and correction.

There is always that unusual circumstance when few if any of the rules seem to apply. When I began working with the retarded, I was not aware there was a five-year-old stripper in the class! The first time I turned from the blackboard and found the little naked figure before me, my mind was bare, too! Ultimately, persistency proved to be the answer. But how many hours it took of redressing that tiny miss, I would not like to estimate.

The letter to the Hebrews sums it all up best, "Now no chastening for the present seemeth to be joyous, but grievous . . . ." If you have ever been faced with a difficult behavior problem, you have experienced the truth of this statement! However, that Scripture goes on to say, ". . . nevertheless afterward it yieldeth the peaceable fruit of righteousness unto them which are exercised thereby."

As the parent or teacher of a retarded child, may God use these thoughts to encourage, direct, and bless you!

If you've just finished this book, we think you'll agree . . .

A COOK PAPERBACK IS

REWARDING READING

Try some more!

(Cont.)

WHAT ABOUT HOROSCOPES? by Joseph Bayly. A topic on everyone's mind! As the author answers the question posed by the title, he also discusses witches, other occult subjects.
51490—95¢

IS THERE HEALING POWER? by Karl Roebling. A keen interest in healing led the author to a quest of facts. A searching look at faith healers: Kathryn Kuhlman, Oral Roberts, others.
68460—95¢

SEX SENSE AND NONSENSE by James Hefley. Just what does the Bible say, and NOT say, about sex? A re-examination of common views—in the light of the Scriptures.
56135—95¢

THE KENNEDY EXPLOSION by E. Russell Chandler. An exciting new method of lay evangelism boosts a tiny Florida church from 17 to 2,450 members. Over 50,000 copies sold.
63610—95¢

STRANGE THINGS ARE HAPPENING by Roger Ellwood. Takes you for a close look at what's happening in the world of Satanism and the occult today . . . and tells what it means.
68478—95¢

You can order these books from your local bookstore, or from the David C. Cook Publishing Co., Elgin, IL 60120 (in Canada: Weston, Ont. M9L 1T4).

-------------**Use This Coupon**-------------

Name _____

Address _____

City _____ State _____ ZIP Code _____

TITLE	STOCK NO.	PRICE	QTY.	ITEM TOTAL
		$		$

Sub-total $ _____

NOTE: On orders placed with David C. Cook Publishing Co., add handling charge of 25¢ for first dollar, plus 5¢ for each additional dollar.

Handling _____

TOTAL $ _____